Behaviour and Process Modelling

London: The Stationery Office

Published with the permission of the Central Computer and Telecommunications Agency on behalf of the Controller of Her Majesty's Stationery Office.

First published 2000

ISBN 0 11 330874 4

Titles within the Business Systems Development series include:

SSADM Foundation	ISBN 0 11 330870 1
Data Modelling	ISBN 0 11 330871 X
The Business Context	ISBN 0 11 330872 8
User Centred Design	ISBN 0 11 330873 6
Behaviour and Process Modelling	ISBN 0 11 330874 4
Function Modelling	ISBN 0 11 330875 2
Database and Physical Process Design	ISBN 0 11 330876 0
Also available as a boxed set	ISBN 0 11 330883 3

For further information on CCTA products
Contact:

CCTA Help Desk
Rosebery Court
St Andrews Business Park
Norwich NR7 0HS
Tel 01603 704567 GTN 3040 4567

CONTENTS

FORWARD

The Business Systems Development (BSD) series represents 'best practice' approaches to investigating, modelling and specifying Information Systems. The techniques described within this series have been used on systems development projects for a number of years and a substantial amount of experience has contributed to the development of this guidance.

Within the BSD series the techniques are organised into groups that cover specific areas of the development process, for example *User Centred Design* which covers all aspects of the investigation, specification and design of the user interface.

The techniques provide a practical approach to the analysis and design of IT systems. They can also be used in conjunction with other complementary techniques such as Object-Oriented techniques.

The material used within this series originated in the Structured Systems Analysis and Design Method (SSADM) which was introduced by the CCTA as a standard method for the development of medium to large IT systems. Since its introduction in the early 1980's, SSADM has been developed through a number of versions to keep pace with the evolving technology and approaches in the IT industry.

The *SSADM Foundation* volume within the BSD series describes the basic concepts of the method and the way in which it can be employed on projects. It also describes how the different techniques can be used in combination. Each of the other volumes in the series describes techniques and approaches for developing elements of the overall specification and design. These can be used in conjunction with one another or as part of alternative approaches. Cross-referencing is provided in outline within the description of each of the techniques to give pointers to the other approaches and techniques that should be considered for use in combination with the one being described.

All volumes within the Business System Development series are available from:

The Stationery Office
St Crispins
Duke Street
Norwich
NR3 1PD

Acknowledgments

Laurence Slater of Slater Consulting Ltd is acknowledged for editing existing material and where necessary developing new material for the volumes within the Business Systems Development series. John Hall, Jennifer Stapleton, Caroline Slater and Ian Clowes are acknowledged for much of the original material on which this series is based.

The following are thanked for their contribution and co-operation in the development of this series:

Paul Turner - Parity Training
Tony Jenkins - Parity Training
Caroline Slater - Slater Consulting Ltd

In addition to those named above a number of people agreed to review aspects of the series and they are thanked accordingly.

1 INTRODUCTION

This volume in the *Business Systems* Development series is concerned with the construction of models which show the system's view of requirements. These models can be divided into two categories:

- **Entity Behaviour Models**, which identify the triggers (events and enquiries) that will cause the system to access its stored data and then show how these triggers affect the stored data over time. This involves the development of an Entity Access Matrix, an Event and Enquiry Catalogue and Entity Life Histories.
- **Conceptual Process Models**, which define the processing requirements for the system which result from the event and enquiry triggers. This involves the development of Enquiry Access Paths (EAPs), Effect Correspondence Diagrams (ECDs), Enquiry Process Models and Update Process Models.

These two areas are very powerful in that they turn the analysis models that have already been produced (e.g., Logical Data Models) into the processing requirements that will need to be developed for the new system. In addition they are very powerful in validating the other models and ensuing they are consistent with one another. One further advantage is that they help to define the "rules" by which the processing is done.

Within Behaviour and Process Modelling, the models that are developed are generally independent of the physical architecture for the new system. This gives a number of advantages, including:

- the models are readable as they are developed to a common standard;
- the architecture of the new system does not need to be fully defined at the time the models are developed;
- the analysts/designers developing the models do not need a deep understanding of the physical architecture of the new system.

In this series all products are shown in the context of the System Development Template (SDT). This is a template which divides the system development process into activity areas onto which the development products can be mapped. Annexe A provides a fuller description of the System Development Template. Figure 1-1 shows how the products of Behaviour and Process Modelling map onto the System Development Template.

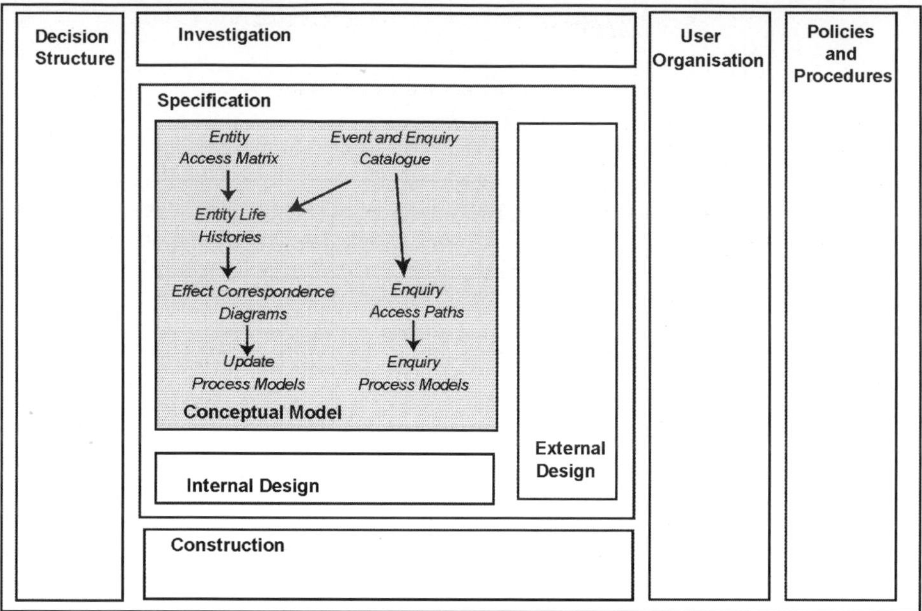

Figure 1-1 Place of Behaviour and Process Modelling Products in the System Development Template

As can be seen from the diagram above all the products covered are contained within the Conceptual Model which is in itself contained within the Specification area of the System Development Template.

Development of the Conceptual Model

Events, enquiries and entities, and their interaction, are essential in specifying the underlying requirements for a system. The techniques that model these elements are central to the Conceptual Model which is in the Specification part of the System Development Template. The context of events, enquiries and entities within Specification is represented in Figure 1-2.

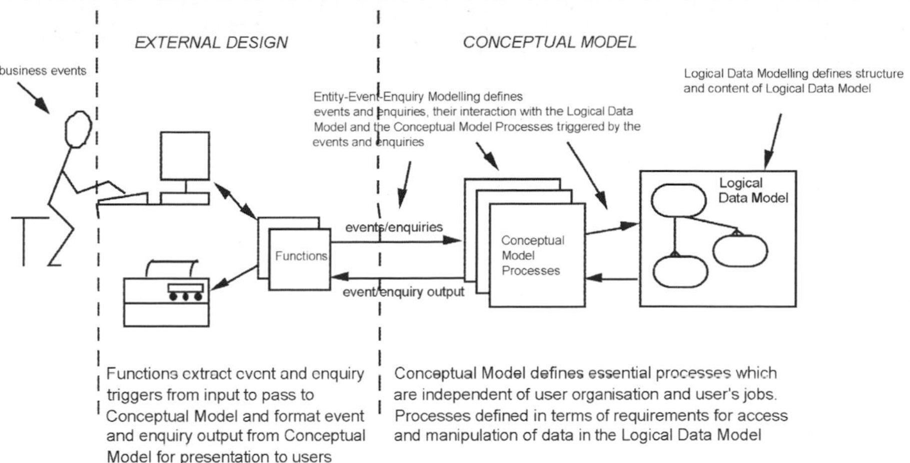

Figure 1-2 Events, enquiries and entities in Specification

There are some important dependencies in the development of products in the Conceptual Model:

- information outputs required by the business are described in the Requirements Catalogue. The Requirements Catalogue will therefore be a key input in the identification of enquiries. The types of information support requirements that may be documented in the Requirements Catalogue include enquiries, reports, prompts and exports to external tools such as spreadsheets;
- these Requirements Catalogue entries are used to validate the Logical Data Model, and help determine its content. The Required System Logical Data Model must be capable of delivering the required information support. If there are any requirements that cannot be supported, the Logical Data Model must be modified. If there are parts of the Logical Data Model that are not used in meeting any defined requirement, their inclusion must be questioned (see the *Data Modelling* volume in this series);
- once the Required System Logical Data Model has been developed with reference to business information requirements, it is possible to analyse it to identify requirements for changes to the data. Since the Logical Data Model directly models the information needed by the business, changes to occurrences of entities in the Logical Data Model should correspond to events that cause change in the business;
- events should be identifiable from business events which cause changes to the states of data in the Conceptual Model. Each event is notified to the system as input via one or more functions. In addition, other models of processing and data can be used to identify the events.

The Conceptual Model is developed by a process of discovery, based on an understanding of business activities and their requirements for information support. When we know what information support is needed for business activities, the Conceptual Model can be developed to ensure that the business activities are supported by the information they require and that data is updated in line with the events which affect the business environment.

Throughout this chapter, a distinction is made between 'business events' and Conceptual Model (CM) events. To avoid confusion between the two terms, the following guidelines should be kept in mind:

- a business event is something that happens in the business context to which the business must react. Business events do not always affect the data held in the automated system. Examples of business events are 'customer arrives' and 'car involved in accident';
- a Conceptual Model event is something that happens in the context of the system to which the system must react by updating data. A business event may be the source of an event that affects the system data but there is not necessarily a one-to-one correspondence between a business event and a Conceptual Model event. For example, in the EU-Rent system, the arrival of a customer in the business can involve a number of business activities unrelated to the automated system before being translated into the Conceptual Model events 'Walk-in Rental' or 'Transfer Pick-up'. Another example is where the business events of 'car involved in accident' and 'car damaged in car park' will translate into a single Conceptual Model event, i.e., 'car damaged'.

As it is the Conceptual Model event that the analyst is ultimately interested in modelling then throughout the rest of this publication a Conceptual Model event will simply be called an *event.*

Logical Data Structure used in examples

Within this volume there are many examples all of which relate to the EU-Rent case study. Both the techniques demonstrated use the Logical Data Model as their base.

Figure 1-3 is the Logical Data Structure for EU-Rent and this will be used throughout this volume.

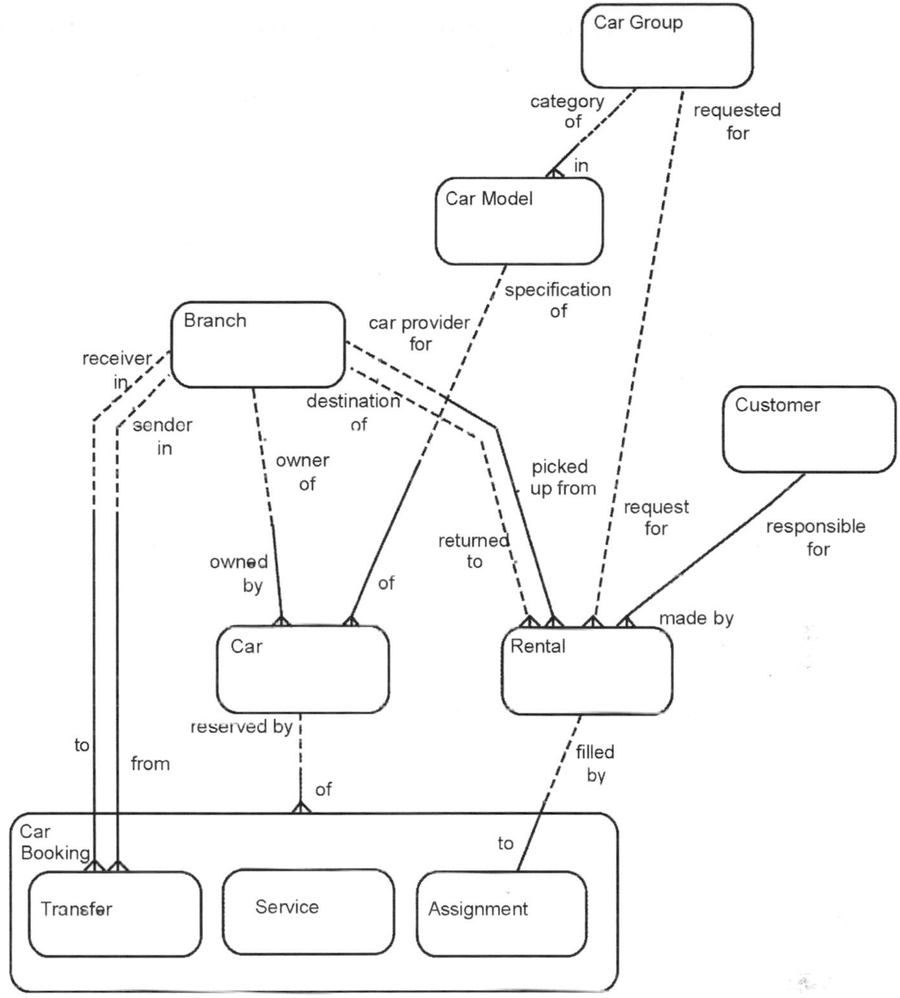

Figure 1-3 EU-Rent Logical Data Structure

Organisation of this volume

After this (introductory) chapter this volume will be structured as follows:

Chapter 2 – Entity Behaviour Modelling. This is a full description of the concepts, products and techniques necessary for the development of the Entity Access Matrix, the Event and Enquiry Matrix and the Entity Life Histories.

Chapter 3 – Conceptual Process Modelling. This is a full description of the concepts, products and techniques necessary for the development of Enquiry Access Paths, Effect Correspondence Diagrams, Enquiry Process Models and Update Process Models.

Chapter 4 – Meta-model. To assist projects to understand the relationship between the concepts used within this volume, a meta-model is provided which shows the basic concepts covered in this volume and way they interrelate.

Chapter 5 – Product Descriptions. Product descriptions are provided for all the major products described in this volume. These should be used by projects as a basis for the product descriptions to be used on the project. (Note: It is expected that the project will need to tailor these product descriptions so that items not required are omitted and any other items required by the project are included.)

Annexes. There are three annexes appended to this volume. The first gives a description of the System Development Template, the second is a description of EU-Rent which is the case study that is used throughout this volume. The third is a glossary of terms that are relevant to this volume.

2 ENTITY BEHAVIOUR MODELLING

Entity Behaviour Modelling covers a set of techniques which model the interaction between data and processes. The techniques of Entity Behaviour Modelling are shown in Figure 2-1 which shows the context of these techniques within the System Development Template.

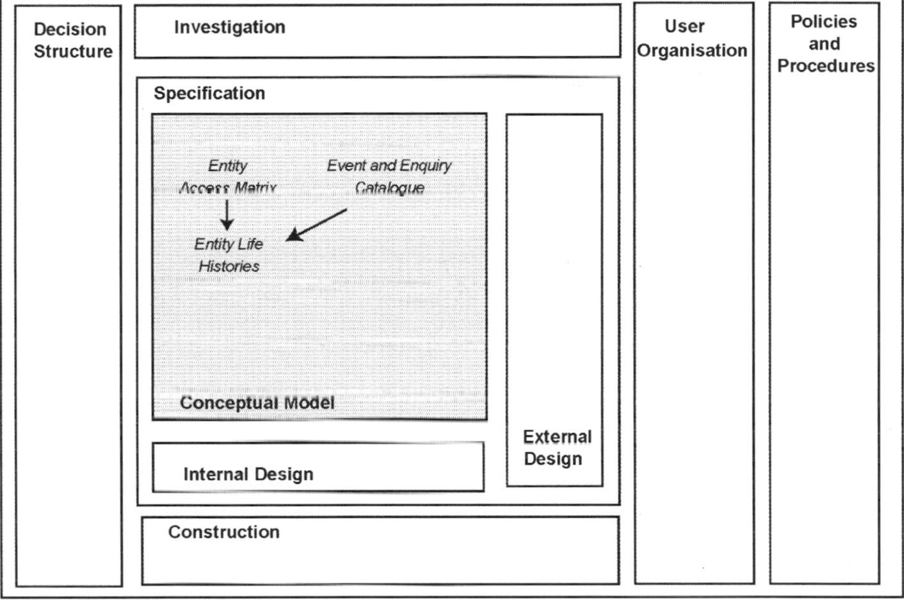

Figure 2-1 Entity Behaviour Modelling in the System Development Template

In this chapter the techniques of Event Identification, Enquiry Identification and Entity Life Histories are described.

Events and enquiries are the building blocks for the specification of processing for the required system. They are the triggers to processes which navigate and manipulate data. Events and enquiries are packaged together by functions. Functions act as a filter between users and events/enquiries in the following way (Figure 1-2):

- functions extract event and enquiry triggers from user input and pass them across to the Conceptual Model;
- functions receive the event and enquiry output and format it for presentation to the user.

Event Identification is a technique which identifies all events by examination of the analysis products defining processing (e.g., Data Flow Model) and those which define data (e.g., Logical Data Model).

Event Identification derives the events of the required system by examining the Required System Data Flow Model and Required System Logical Data Model. The identification of events can be done in parallel with the identification of functions. Business Activity Models (see *The Business Context* volume in this series) will also help in the identification of business events which may correspond to events that cause changes to the Conceptual Model data.

Enquiry Identification is a technique which identifies all enquiries by examining the information support requirements for business activities and from user requirements. Enquiries are used to help build and validate the Logical Data Model (see the *Data Modelling* volume in this series). Enquiries are identified by consideration of the information support requirements for business activities.

The Entity Life History Analysis technique, which is regarded as a major analysis and design technique, is used to model the sequence of events which affect specific entities on the Required System Logical Data Model. This is done in order to define constraints on the updating of entities and to explore the required degree to which business events and business rules are reflected in requirements for updating of data within the system. The results of Entity Life History Analysis are fed into Conceptual Process Modelling (see Chapter 3).

Event Identification, Enquiry Identification and Entity Life History Analysis help to validate and enhance the products of Function Definition and Logical Data Modelling.

Events and enquiries are cross-referenced to entities on the Required System Logical Data Model using the Entity Access Matrix.

Events and enquiries are documented. The product which may be used to document events and enquiries is the Event and Enquiry Catalogue.

The Entity Life History Analysis technique is used to investigate the lives of entities, identifying the events which affect their lives, documenting the way in which the lives are affected and showing the sequence in which the effects take place. The major operations for each effect are identified.

2.1 Concepts of Entity Behaviour Modelling

2.1.1 Business Event

A business event is something that happens in the business context to which the business must react. Business events do not always affect the data held in the automated system. Examples of business events are ‘customer arrives’ and ‘car involved in accident’.

2.1.2 Event (also known as Conceptual Model Event)

An event is something that triggers a Conceptual Model process to update the system data. It is usually sourced by a business event, notified to the system via one or more functions. An event provides the reason for an update process to be initiated. The name of the event should be a noun clause and should reflect what is causing the process to be invoked – not the process name itself. Typical event names might include terms such as 'Receipt', 'Notification', 'Decision', 'Arrival', 'New', 'Change'.

2.1.3 Enquiry

An enquiry is something that triggers a Conceptual Model process to extract information from the system data without updating the data in any way.

2.1.4 Entity Life History

An Entity Life History (ELH) charts all of the events that may cause a particular entity occurrence to change in some way and places them in sequence.

An Entity Life History is a structured diagram showing a combination of all possible lives for every occurrence of an entity. Each occurrence is constrained to act in the way defined by the Entity Life History for that entity.

2.1.5 Effect

The change within a single entity occurrence caused by an event is called an effect.

Each effect is documented on the Entity Life History diagram for the relevant entity. Effects are represented on the Entity Life Histories as boxes and are shown by the name of the event. Effects are at the bottom of the Entity Life History structure.

2.1.6 Effect Qualifiers

An occurrence of an entity may be affected in one of several mutually exclusive ways by an event. A single occurrence of an event will result in only one type of effect. Each possible effect is separately identified on the Entity Life History diagram by using the event name followed by a description of the effect enclosed in round brackets.

2.1.7 Entity Role

If a single occurrence of an event affects more than one occurrence of a particular entity and the effects are different, the entity has a different role for each different type of effect. Entity roles are identified by adding them to effect boxes on the Entity Life History enclosed in square brackets. An effect can have both an entity role and an effect qualifier but is more likely to have either one or the other.

2.1.8 Super-event

If several different events have exactly the same effects on an entity at the same point in its life, the effects can be called by a name which describes them all – this is the super-event name. If the same set of events appears in another Entity Life History, again with the same effects, the individual effects do not need to be shown – instead the super-event name can be used. In Effect Correspondence Diagrams (see Chapter 3), the super-events become common processes which are 'called' by each event included in the super-event. Super-events are documented on the Entity Access Matrix, are described in the Event and Enquiry Catalogue and are modelled using Effect Correspondence Diagrams.

2.1.9 Common Enquiry

A common enquiry is an enquiry which is only ever invoked by other enquiries or events. It is defined and documented separately as an enquiry and invoked by the other enquiries and/or events that use it. Each common enquiry should be identified and documented in the same way as all other enquiries. Common enquiries are modelled using Enquiry Access Paths.

2.1.10 Death vs. Deletion

Note that the effects termed 'death' within this chapter do not necessarily imply deletion. Events causing an entity's death move the entity to a state in which it no longer has any active role within the system. The events causing the deletion of the entity will depend upon the archive strategy and, in some situations, may be determined simply by how much physical space is available for the database. Unless thought useful there is no necessity to reflect events which cause deletion on each Entity Life History – the deletion events may not be known at the point of Entity Life History Analysis.

2.2 Products of Entity Behaviour Modelling

The products of Entity Behaviour Modelling are as follows:

- Entity Access Matrix;
- Event and Enquiry Catalogue;
- Entity Life Histories.

The Entity Access Matrix, Event and Enquiry Catalogue and Entity Life History products are described further in the following paragraphs.

2.2.1 Entity Access Matrix

The Entity Access Matrix is a powerful working document that helps to identify which entities are affected or accessed by a particular event or enquiry.

Entities (including entity aspects and sub/super types) from the Required System Logical Data Model are placed along one axis of the matrix, and events and enquiries are placed along the other axis as they are discovered. Intersections of the matrix are completed to indicate the type of access. If an event accesses an entity in several different ways (possibly in different contexts), several entries can be made in a single intersection of the matrix.

Super-events and common enquiries identified during Entity Behaviour Modelling are documented on the Entity Access Matrix as well as events and enquiries.

There are no specific notational conventions for an Entity Access Matrix: the precise format will depend upon the tools available to the project. An example Entity Access Matrix developed for the EU-Rent system is shown in Figure 2-2.

ENTITIES EVENTS/ENQUIRIES	Car Booking	Car Booking: Transfer	Car Booking Assignment	Branch	Car	Car Model
EVENTS:						
Car Allocation to Rental	I, T		I, T		G	R
Rental Pick-up	M		M			
Rental Return	M		M	G,L	M, T, C	
Transfer Pick-up	M	M		X	M, S	
Walk-in Rental	I,T		I, T		G	
Car Model Death					D,C	D, C
ENQUIRIES:						
Car Availability					R	R
Customer History	R			R	R	R
Unallocated Bookings	R			R		R

Figure 2-2 Extract from an Entity Access Matrix

The key to the entries in the intersections of the matrix is as follows (note that not all of these categories will be required for all projects):

- **I: insert**. An 'I' indicates that an occurrence of this event causes the insertion, or creation, of one or more occurrences of this entity;
- **M: modify**. An 'M' indicates that an occurrence of this event causes attributes to be changed within one or more occurrences of this entity;

- **R: read**. An 'R' indicates that each occurrence of this event or enquiry accesses one or more occurrences of this entity for the purpose of determining attribute values or as part of a navigation path around the Logical Data Model.
- **D: death**. A 'D' indicates that an occurrence of this event causes the death of one or more occurrences of this entity (i.e., the entity occurrences have no further active role to play in the system but they may still be available for enquiries);
- **B: 'buried' (delete)**. A 'B' indicates that an occurrence of this event causes the deletion of one or more occurrences of the entity (i.e., the entity occurrences are no longer recognised by the system);
- **G: gain detail**. A 'G' indicates that an occurrence of this event causes one or more occurrences of a detail entity to be linked via a relationship to one or more occurrences of this entity. A 'G' should always have one or more corresponding 'T' entries for the associated detail entities;
- **L: lose detail**. An 'L' indicates that an occurrence of this event causes one or more occurrences of a detail entity to be detached from one or more occurrences of this entity by the severance of relationships. An 'L' should always have one or more corresponding 'C' entries for the associated detail entities;
- **T: tie**. A 'T' indicates that each occurrence of this event causes one or more occurrences of this entity to be linked to an occurrence of a master entity via a relationship. This would be represented by the assignment of a value to the foreign key. A 'T' may have one or more corresponding 'G' entries for the master entities;
- **C: cut**. A 'C' indicates that each occurrence of this event causes one or more occurrences of this entity to be detached from an occurrence of a master entity by deleting a relationship. This would be represented by assigning 'null' values to the foreign key. A 'C' may have one or more corresponding 'L' entries for the master entities;
- **X: swap detail(s) between occurrences**. An 'X' indicates that an occurrence of this event causes occurrences of a detail entity to be swapped from one occurrence of this entity to another by the severance of one relationship and the creation of another relationship. An 'X' may have one or more corresponding 'S' entries for the detail entities;
- **S: swap master(s) between occurrences**. An 'S' indicates that each occurrence of this event causes one or more occurrences of this entity to be detached from one occurrence of a master entity and attached to another occurrence of the master by deleting and creating relationships. This would be represented by altering values of the foreign key. An 'S' may have one or more corresponding 'X' entries for the master entities;

For events it is possible to have all the different types of operation. For enquiries, it is only possible to have the Read operation. The first four entry types (Insert, Modify, Read and Deletion) are the major types and the analyst should make every effort to get these types correctly cross-referenced on the matrix.

Not all entries need to be carried forward to Entity Life Histories and Conceptual Process Modelling techniques. The apparent duplication between entries such as Gain and Tie is necessary in order to be precise about which relationships are being affected by a particular event. In Entity Life Histories and beyond, a choice may be made to model these changes from the point of view of the detail entity alone as operations will identify the masters affected.

2.2.2 Event and Enquiry Catalogue

The Event and Enquiry Catalogue records information about the important characteristics of each event and enquiry. The Event and Enquiry Catalogue is likely to be in the form of a report from a CASE tool, so it is not possible to be precise about its format or content. Instead, the Event and Enquiry Catalogue is described in terms of the information that needs to be recorded. This information should be available to analysts from whatever tools are used within the project.

Super-events and common enquiries should be documented in the Event and Enquiry Catalogue and cross-referenced to their corresponding events and enquiries.

It should be noted that some of the information listed below duplicates information that is present on the Entity Access Matrix, Entity Life Histories, Enquiry Access Paths and Effect Correspondence Diagrams. If a CASE tool is available that captures information from these other products automatically, this information does not need to be recorded separately but should still be available for interrogation. The Event and Enquiry Catalogue is simply a view of the information collected by the CASE tool.

The information that should be recorded for each event and enquiry includes the following:

Property	Description
Event/enquiry name	The unique and generally agreed name for the event/enquiry being described.
Event/enquiry ID	A short reference name or number for the event/enquiry (optional).
Event/enquiry description	A definitive statement of the significance of the event/enquiry within the system. This should help readers to visualise occurrences.
Business activity/event	References to business activities or business events from which event notification is obtained (events) or information support is required (enquiries).
Average occurrences	An estimate of the average number of occurrences of the event/enquiry in a particular period (e.g., 10 per day). Any assumptions made in estimating the average should also be recorded.
Maximum occurrences	An estimate of the maximum number of occurrences of the event/enquiry in a particular period (e.g., 100 per hour). Any assumptions made in estimating the maximum should

be recorded. Also, if the maximum occurs only during specified periods, these should be documented (e.g., from 9am to 10am)

Data required as input to the event/enquiry A list of attributes required for the event/enquiry to identify occurrences of entities in the Logical Data Model and provide values for attributes (events) so that the triggered Conceptual Model Process can be executed.

Entry point to the logical data model The entity from the Logical Data Model which will be the first entity accessed by this event or enquiry.

Entities accessed A list of the entities accessed – and the access type – can be derived from the Entity Access Matrix.

Sample entries from the Event and Enquiry Catalogue are shown in Figure 2-3 and Figure 2-4. As can be seen from these examples, the entries can be different for the different types.

Event name	Delivery	Event ID	C017
Event description	A new car is delivered and added to the stock of its model at the receiving branch.		
Business activity/event	Car delivery from manufacturer.		
Average Occurrences	Airport branch (100): 700 per year City branch (200): 375 per year Local Agency branch (700): 80 per year Total per year		70,000 75,000 56,000 —— 201,000
Maximum Occurrences	Evenly spread over the year in normal working hours, in groups of 6 (airport and city branches) and 2 (local agencies).		
Data required as input to the event	Car registration number, purchase reference, model id, delivery date, kilometres, branch id		
Entry point to the Logical Data Model	Delivery		
Entities accessed	Entity Delivery Car Stock		Access Type Modify Insert Modify

Event name	Rental Return	Event ID	R034
Event description	Check-in of a car at the end of a rental. The charges are calculated and charged to the customer's credit card, and the details are output. If the rental was points-based under the benefits scheme, the points are charged to the customer's benefit account; only extras (e.g. insurance, fuel) are charged to the customer's credit card. If the rental was paid, and the customer is in the benefits scheme, the points earned are credited to the customer's benefit account. If the rental was one-way, ownership of the car is transferred to the drop-off branch.		
Business activity/event	Return of car from rental.		
Average Occurrences	Airport branch (100): 200 per day over 24 hours, 7 days per week. City branch (200): 120 per day over 11 hours, 6 days per week. Local agency branch (700): 30 per day over 11 hours, 6 days per week.		
Maximum Occurrences	Airport branch (100): 30 per hour between 5 p.m. and 8 p.m. City branch (200): 40 per hour between 5 p.m. and 7 p.m. Local agency branch (700): 10 per hour between 5 p.m. and 7 p.m.		
Data required as input to the event	Car registration number, check-in time and date, kilometres, fuel reading, drop-off branch id.		
Entry point to the Logical Data Model	Car		
Entities accessed	Entities Car Stock Car Booking Rental Customer Annual Benefit		Access Type Read/Modify Modify/Death Read/Modify Read/Modify Read Insert/Modify/Death

Figure 2-3 Example entries from Event Catalogue

Enquiry name	Available benefit	Enquiry ID	R062
Enquiry description	When a customer applies for a free rental, his benefit account is checked to see if he has sufficient points to afford it.		
Business activity/event	Rental reservation.		
Average Occurrences	Airport branch (100): 8 per day. City branch (200): 6 per day. Local agency branch (700): ~1 per day.		
Maximum Occurrences	At popular holiday destinations, up to 25 per day for New Year, Easter and mid-July to early August.		
Data required as input to the enquiry	Driver id.		
Entities accessed	Customer.		

Figure 2-4 Example entry from the Enquiry Catalogue

2.2.3 Entity Life History

An Entity Life History (ELH) is a diagram which charts the life of an entity from birth to death within a system in terms of the events which affect it. An Entity Life History is a model of what can happen to entity occurrences over time, and is read from left to right in chronological order of events.

Entity Life Histories use Jackson-like notation with sequences, selections, iterations and parallel structures as the basic structure components. Operations can be added to the bottom boxes of the structure (effects) and state indicators are added below these to indicate the status of the entity at any point in its life.

These basic conventions are summarised in Figure 2-5.

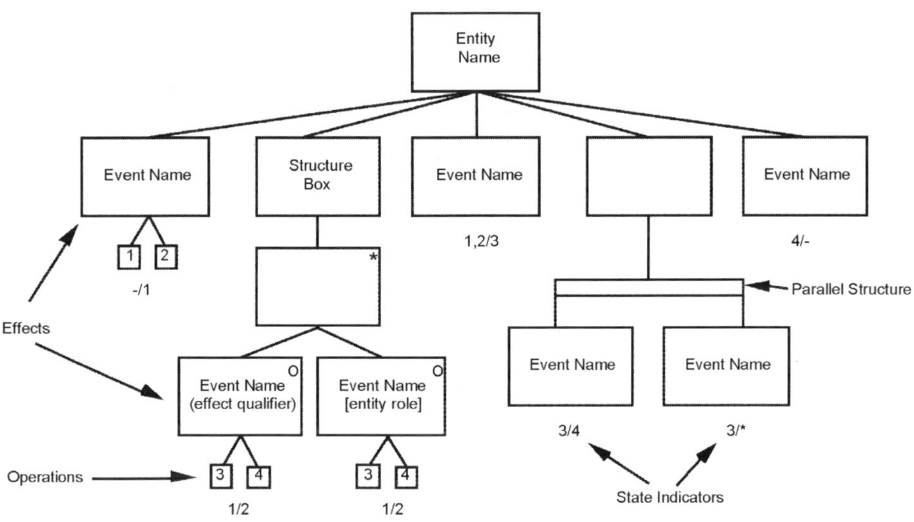

Figure 2-5 Basic conventions for Entity Life Histories

All boxes on the diagram are 'hard' boxes. The top box of the structure contains the name of the entity for which this diagram is drawn. The basic structure contains the following components:

- sequence;
- iteration;
- selection;
- state indicators;
- quit and resume;
- operations;

- parallel structure.

These conventions are described in more detail in the following paragraphs, illustrated with examples taken from the EU-Rent system.

Sequence

A sequence is read from left to right in chronological order. An example of a sequence is shown in Figure 2-6.

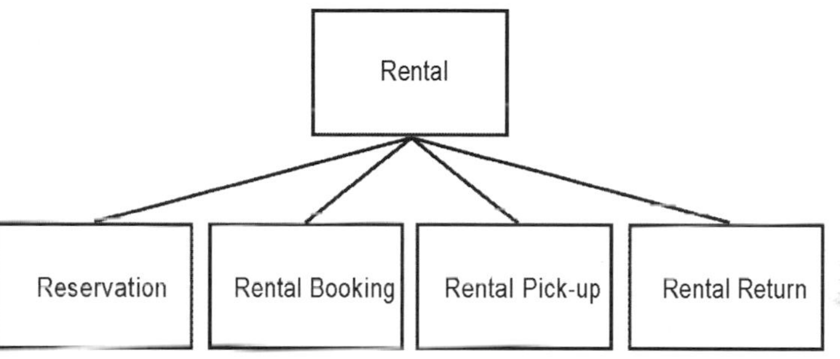

Figure 2-6 Rental ELH showing sequence

This description of a Rental says that it is created when a Reservation is made, and is 'logically dead' (can be physically deleted at any convenient time after this) when Rental Return occurs. During its life, there will be one Rental Booking (when a specific car is assigned to the Rental) and one Rental Pick up. The sequence shows that the booking must happen before the pick-up which must happen before Rental Return.

Selection

A selection defines a number of options at a certain point in an Entity Life History. Each option is indicated with a small circle in the top right corner of the structure component box. An example of a selection is given in Figure 2-7.

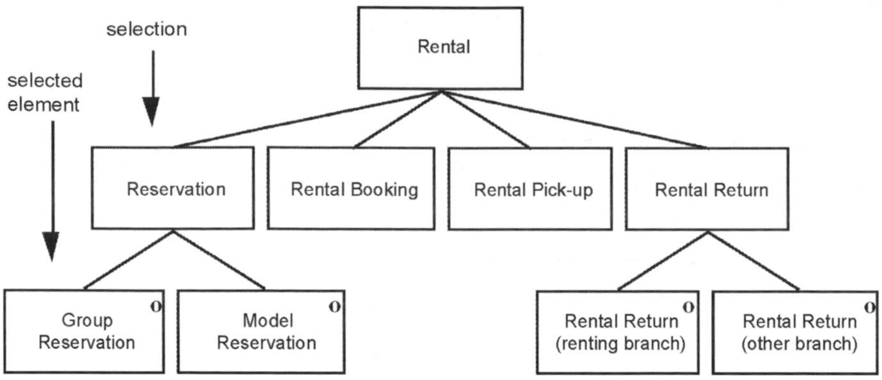

Figure 2-7 Rental ELH showing sequence and selections

This description of Rental says that it is created when either a Group Reservation (requesting a car in a particular price group), or a Model Reservation (requesting a car of a specific model) is made. As above, it is 'logically dead' when the Rental Return is notified. But Rental Return may have two different effects. Either, the car is returned to the renting branch, or it is dropped off at some other branch, in which case ownership is transferred to the drop-off branch and the renting branch is notified.

This diagram also introduces the notation for different effects of the same event – an effect qualifier in parentheses after the event name. Note that different effects of the same event type do not have to appear under a selection; they may be in different parts of the structure. This will be demonstrated in later examples.

The criterion for deciding whether to define different events or different effects of the same event is:

- if it is possible to determine from the input that different processing is needed, define different events. For example, the input for a reservation states whether a model or a car group is requested, so different events are defined;
- if the content of the entity has to be examined in order to decide what processing to do, define different effects of the same event. For example, when a car is dropped off at a branch, the Rental entity has to be examined to see whether the renting branch is the same as the drop-off branch, in order to decide what to do.

One option of a selection must be taken in every case. If it is possible for no event to occur, there must be an explicit null option (a selected component with a dash) shown on the structure. An example of a null selection is given in Figure 2-8.

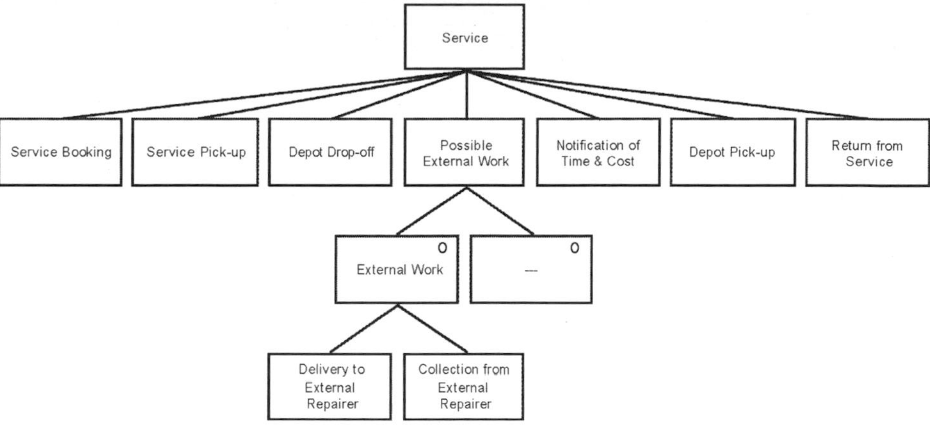

Figure 2-8 Service ELH with null selection

This description of a car service shows that the car may or may not be put out to an external repairer for some of the work.

Iteration

An iteration defines a repeated part of the structure, which may be a single event or a substructure. The iterated component has an asterisk in the upper right corner of the structure component box. An example of an iteration is given in Figure 2-9.

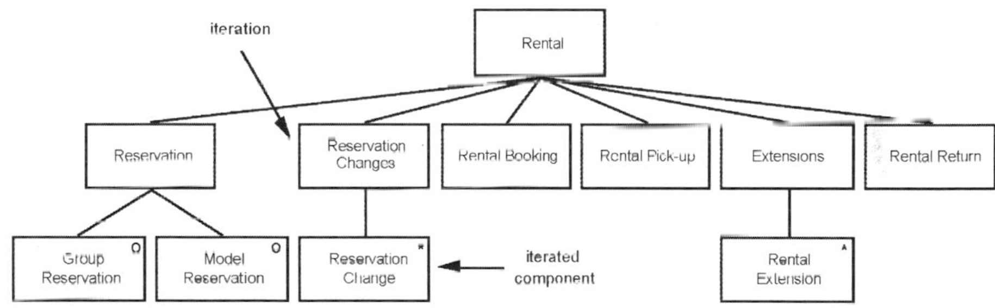

Figure 2-9 Rental ELH with iterations

This description of Rental says that at any time before Rental Booking (when a specific car is assigned) the reservation details may be changed, any number of times, including zero. Similarly, after the car has been picked up, any number of Rental Extensions may be made but not after the car has been returned.

Note that what we are modelling is the system's view of events. For example, the customer may request a rental extension that EU-Rent refuses; this business event is not reflected in the Entity Life History since there is no requirement to record the refused request in the system.

Parallel structures

Some entities may be affected by several different sets of events which are unrelated and will happen in parallel with one another. For example, in the EU-Rent system, the following two parallel sets of events may affect the entity Customer:

- a customer may be suspended for a period by EU-Rent management. Until the suspension is lifted, the customer cannot rent any cars. This can be modelled on the Entity Life History by showing a sequence of Customer Suspension and Customer Reinstatement, with no Walk-in Rentals or Reservations between them;
- EU-Rent wants to be able to record comments about customers, and to change personal details such as addresses and telephone numbers at any time, whether or not the customer is suspended.

The parallel notation used on Entity Life Histories illustrated in Figure 2-10 illustrates this.

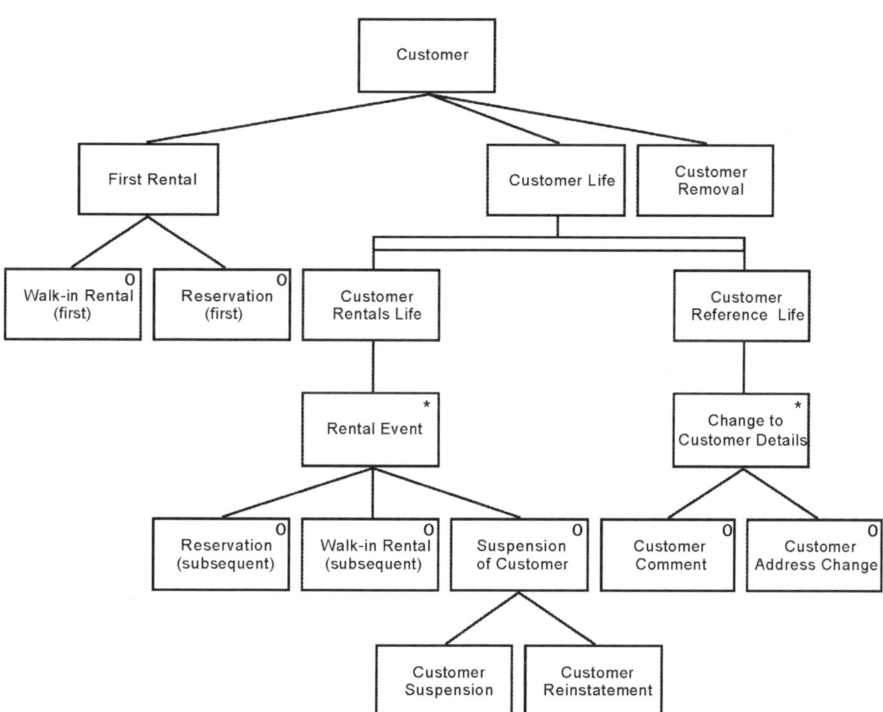

Figure 2-10 Parallel structure on Customer Entity Life History

In many cases, this kind of requirement will be resolved by splitting the entity into separate aspects, one aspect being subject to one of the parallel lives and the other being subject to another parallel life (see *Data Modelling* in this series). The parallel life notation is useful for simpler cases where the split into aspects is not justified.

Combining the elements

Combinations of the structure components are used to build Entity Life Histories as large and as complex (or as small and as simple) as are needed to describe entity behaviour. For example, the Entity Life History in Figure 2-11 shows the Rental entity's behaviour extended to allow walk-in rentals as well as advance reservations.

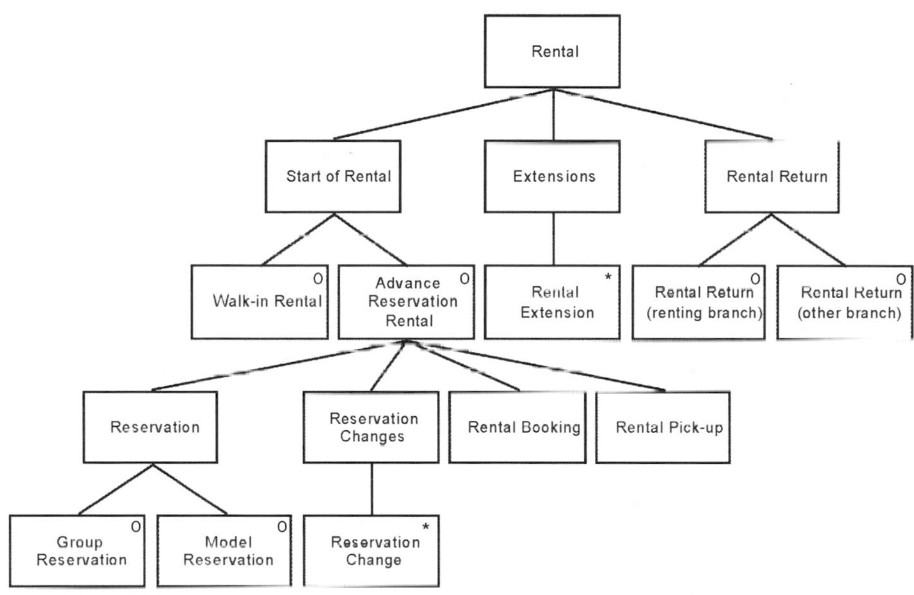

Figure 2-11 Rental ELH extended to show Walk-in Rentals

Each non-leaf structure component, whether it is the entity (the top box) or an intermediate component, must be a sequence, a selection, an iteration or a parallel structure node. This means that the components immediately beneath a non-leaf structure component must all be of the same type, for example, elements of a sequence, options if a selection, or a single iterated component. The diagram in Figure 2-12 is meaningless in terms of Entity Life History syntax.

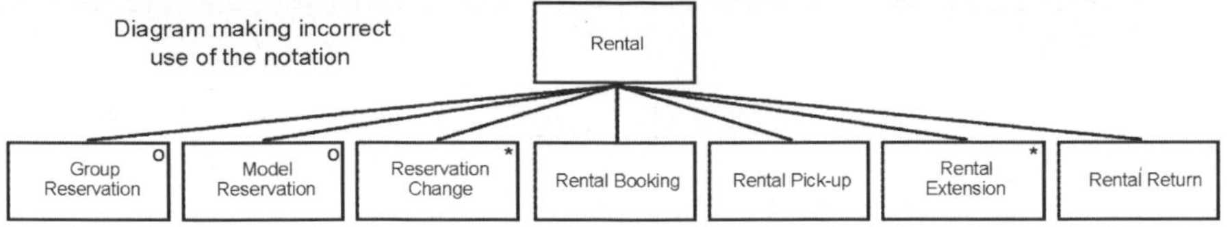

Figure 2-12 Example of incorrect syntax for Entity Life Histories

In this diagram, Rental is not a sequence, a selection or an iteration. The diagram is not a valid Entity Life History.

State Indicators

Each entity has a state indicator, updated each time an event causes an update to the entity's data. A state indicator can be thought of as an additional attribute within each entity which can be used to ascertain where, in the entity's life history this occurrence is and can be documented within the Entity Description as an attribute where required. Where there is a need to record that an event has occurred, the state indicator is automatically updated to a new value.

Inspection of the state indicator value of an entity occurrence at any one time will identify where a the entity occurrence is within its life, and determine which event(s) may next update the entity occurrence. The validation logic implicit in the state indicators can be carried forward into process design.

State indicators can be used to validate the structure of an Entity Life History. The state indicator values should be consistent with the structure of the Entity Life History diagram.

The state indicator notation on an Entity Life History is generally of the format 'number(s)/number' where:

- the numbers prior to the slash identify the permitted values of the state indicator prior to its update by the relevant effect;
- the number after the slash represents the value of the state indicator once it has been updated by a particular effect.

If in checking the state indicator, the current value is not equal to one of the values of the prior permitted states, the effect cannot take place and exception processing can be invoked.

The value assigned to a state indicator is only meaningful within the context of one Entity Life History; there is no need to relate the state indicator to any other effects on other diagrams.

For events which create an occurrence of an entity, there will obviously be no previous valid value for the state indicator. In such instances, the previous valid value of the state indicator is deemed to be 'null' and is represented on the diagram as '-', i.e., the state indicator for an event creating an occurrence of an entity would be in the format '-/number'.

Similarly for events which will delete an occurrence of an entity, the state indicator will need to be set to the same null value, i.e., the state indicator for an event deleting an occurrence of an entity would be in the format 'number(s)/-' .

The default approach to adding state indicators to Entity Life Histories is that each individual effect sets the state indicator to a different value. An example of an Entity Life History with state indicators added is shown in Figure 2-13.

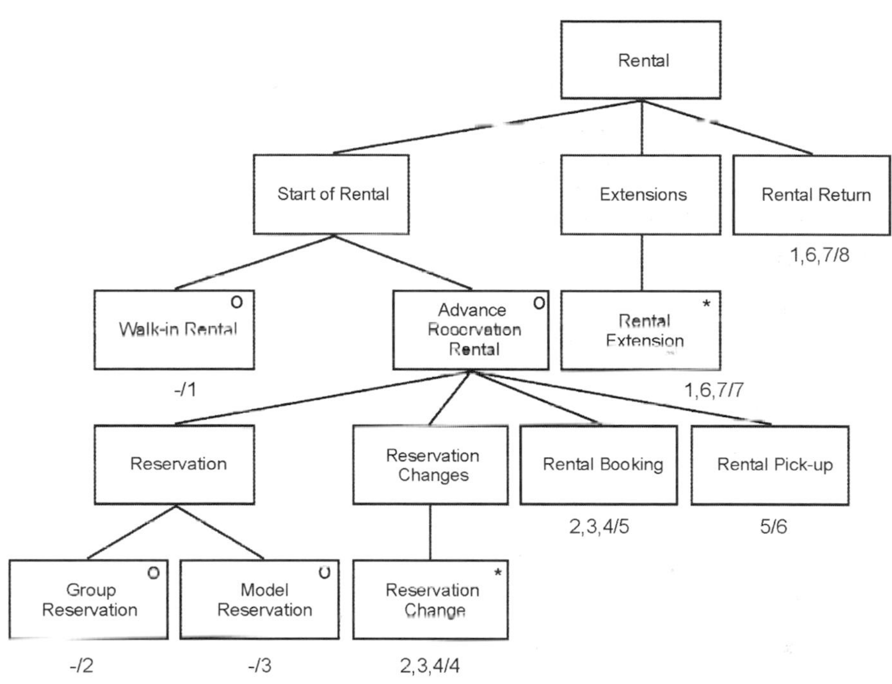

Figure 2-13 Addition of state indicators to Rental ELH (unique values for states)

In this description of Rental (with Rental Return simplified), the state indicator value after each effect is noted under the effect, after the slash. Before the slash is the list of state indicator values that the entity may have for the event to be accepted. For example, a reservation change will be accepted only if the affected instance of Rental is in states 2, 3 or 4, i.e., if the previous event was a Group Reservation, Model Reservation or an earlier Reservation change.

The individual components have state indicators applied as follows:

- for a sequence of effects, the state indicator value set by an effect becomes the valid previous value of the subsequent effect, for example, the effect of the event Rental

Booking sets the state indicator to '5' in the above example and the only valid previous value for the subsequent effect (Rental Pick-up) is '5';

- for a selection of effects, each must have the same set of valid previous state indicator values. The 'set to' values for the selected components are set to a different value unless states are optimised (see below). State indicators under a selection are demonstrated in the example above by Group Reservation and Model Reservation, each of which has the valid previous state of '-'. In this example, each leg of the selection sets the state indicator value to a different value, '2' and '3'. For the effect which follows a selection, the valid previous values must include the state indicator value set by each of the alternative effects (see Reservation Change). Moreover, if these alternative effects include a 'null' box, the valid previous values of the alternative effects must also be included as valid previous values of the subsequent effect (note that the 'null box' is not annotated with state indicator values as it represents the absence of an effect and therefore never happens);
- for an iteration, the set of valid previous values must include the value set by the iterated effect itself. The 'set to' value is a different value from the first valid previous value unless states are optimised (see below). State indicators under an iteration are demonstrated in the example above by Reservation Change which sets the state indicator value to '4' and '4' is also one of its valid previous values. Note that the valid previous values for an iteration are the same as the valid previous values for the effect following the iteration (Rental Booking). This is because the iteration may be zero.

Only one leg of a parallel structure can update the value of the main state indicator (called the 'primary' state indicator). All other legs of the structure leave the primary state indicator unchanged.

There are two choices for the other legs of the parallel structure:

- none of the legs updates a state indicator of any sort;
- if there is a need to monitor the events in any of these legs, each leg updates its own subsidiary state indicator.

To maintain the subsidiary state indicator, the same conventions apply as for the primary state indicator. The subsidiary state indicator is usually set back to 'null' by the first effect following the parallel structure.

State indicators for parallel structures are demonstrated in Figure 2-14.

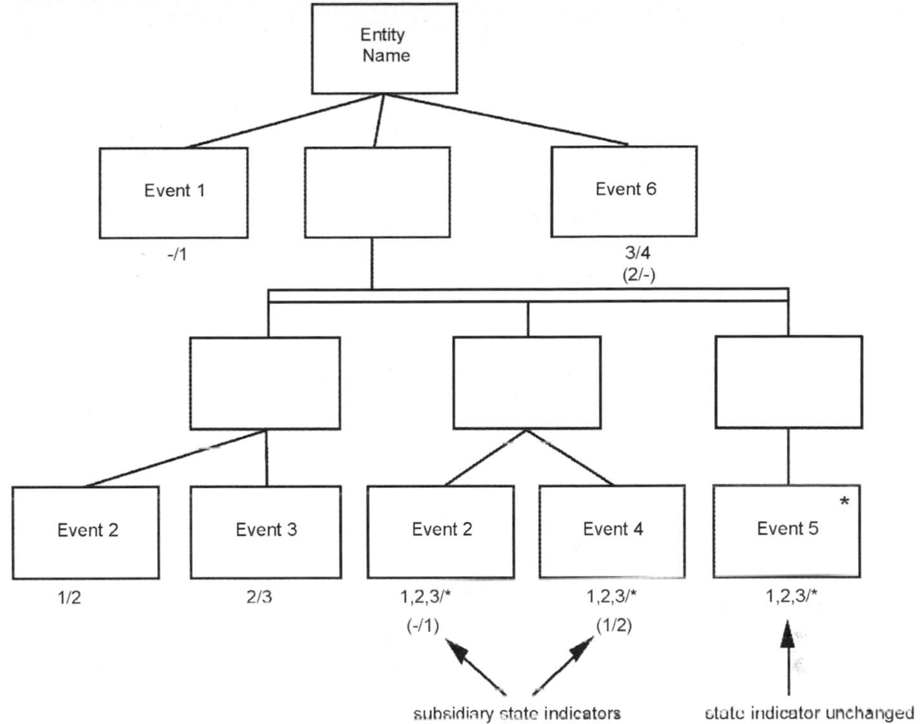

Figure 2-14 State indicators – parallel structures

Note that the asterisk (*) for the set-to value in the primary state indicator means that this state indicator is not altered by this event.

Optimisation of State Indicators

State indicator values can be optimised using two simple guidelines:

- the 'set to' values for the state indicator for each option of a selection can be made the same;
- the 'set to' values for the state indicator for an iterated component can be made the same as the state before the iteration (i.e., the iterated effect does not update the value of the state indicator).

If these guidelines are applied to the example in Figure 2-13, the state indicator values are changed to those shown in Figure 2-15.

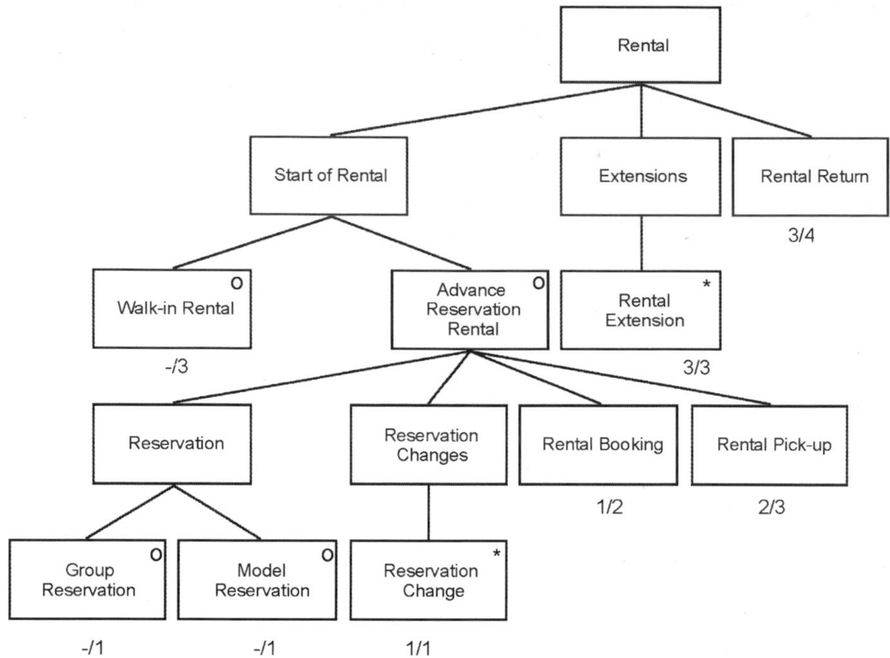

Figure 2-15 Rental ELH with optimised states

Optimisation of states provides three benefits:

- it simplifies testing of the validity of events, giving shorter lists of valid previous state indicator values for subsequent effects;
- it increases reusability of processes, allowing the identification of super-events (see below);
- it supports the naming of states in terms that are meaningful to users. For the example above, the state values mean:

  1 requested (waiting for car to be assigned);

  2 booked (waiting for car to be picked up);

  3 in progress;

  4 completed (waiting to be deleted).

The optimisation of state indicator values is not straightforward where a 'null' selection is used or where certain combinations of selections and iterations are used. One example of a situation where state indicator values should not be optimised is when the final component of an option of a selection is an iteration. This is demonstrated in Figure 2-16.

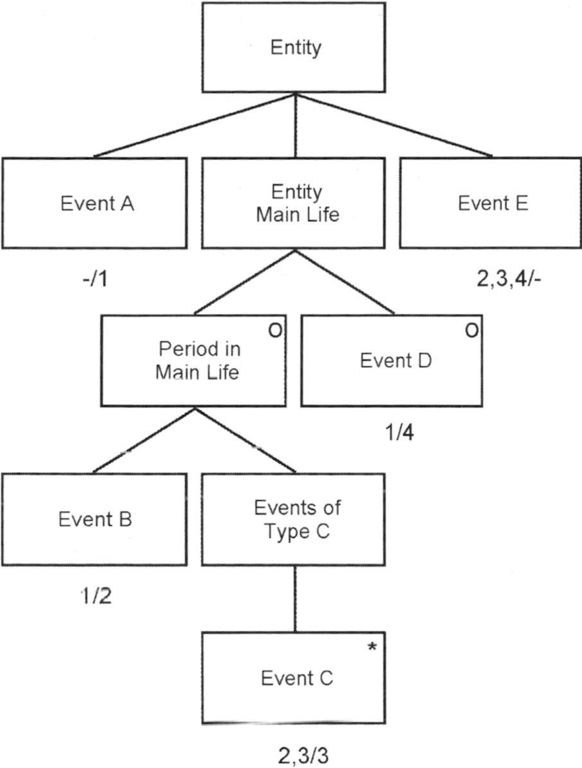

Figure 2-16 Example of state indicators on iteration at end of structure under selection

In the example above, the effects of Event C and Event D are effectively two components of a selection. However, if the same 'set to' state indicator value is given to the effects of Event C and Event D, an iteration of Event C after Event D would be permitted. This contradicts the structure of the Entity Life History and would therefore be an undesirable situation. In all cases, state indicator values should be consistent with the Entity Life History structure.

Quit and Resume convention

The use of Quit and Resume helps the analyst separate out alternative patterns in an Entity Life History, each of which starts the same way. The use of this approach in drawing Entity Life Histories means that an Entity Life History can be built up incrementally, with the normal pattern of events being explored first and alternatives added in later. Both assumed and alternative cases start the same way – the system cannot recognise at the outset whether a reservation will be successful or whether it will be cancelled.

Quits and Resumes are used to jump from an 'assumed case' to an 'alternative case'. The assumed case is always visited first on the Entity Life History. When an event occurs which shows that the Entity Life History should be in the alternative case, a Quit occurs to the appropriate part of the alternative case .

A Quit is denoted by a 'Q' followed by an integer inside or near one or more boxes. A Resume is denoted by an 'R' followed by an integer inside or near a single box. Thus, several Quits – or exits – may lead to the same resumption point. They will be linked by the same numeric identifier. The effect denoted by the R happens instead of the effect(s) denoted by the equivalent Q.

Quits and Resumes can only be used in specific circumstances:

- from one side of a selection to the other;
- from out of an iteration into the main structure of the Entity Life History;
- from anywhere within an Entity Life History structure to an off-the-structure box which represents an effect of an event (or group of effects) which can happen at a random point in the life of the entity.

In general Entity Life History structures should be drawn without the use of Quits and Resumes where possible.

In the EU-Rent System, the normal course of events for a Rental is that a reservation is accepted, the car is picked up and finally returned. However, there will be a proportion of reservations that are cancelled. When any particular reservation arrives, EU-Rent does not know whether the rental will be completed or cancelled. Once the Rental Booking has been made, the car will either be picked up or the rental will be cancelled. The system must accommodate both possibilities. The Quit and Resume structure for Rental is shown in Figure 2-17.

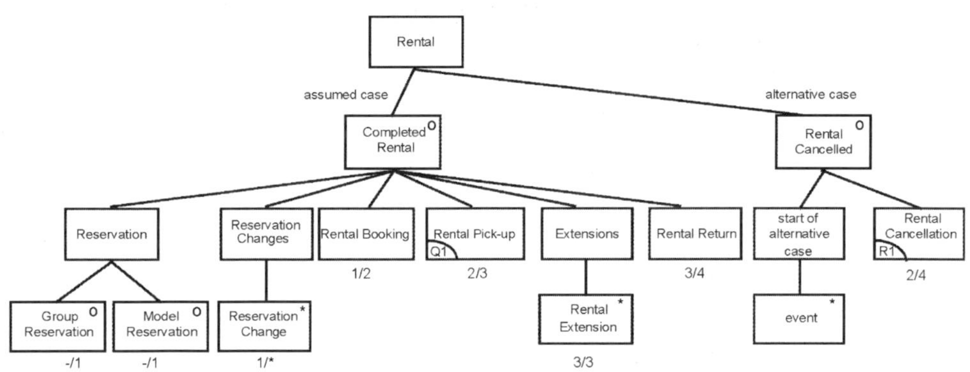

Figure 2-17 Rental Entity Life History with Quit and Resumes

The assumed case for Rental is that the rental will be completed. The point at which the assumption may be proven wrong is marked with a 'Q' (Quit), and the effect of the event which proves it wrong is marked with an 'R' (Resume) in the alternative case.

This Entity Life History appears to have assumed and alternative cases starting in different ways; they actually start the same way, but the Entity Life History would become large and unwieldy if the complete structure of the assumed case before the quit were to be to duplicated under the alternative case. For this reason, a 'shorthand' notation has been used which represents this duplicated part of the structure by a simple iteration of 'event'. Thus, in this example, the iterated 'event' represents the effects of Group Reservation, Model Reservation, Reservation Change and Rental Booking.

This example can be extended to take in the possibility that the rental could be cancelled instead of Reservation Change or Rental Booking. Quits can be added to a number of points in the assumed case as shown in Figure 2-18.

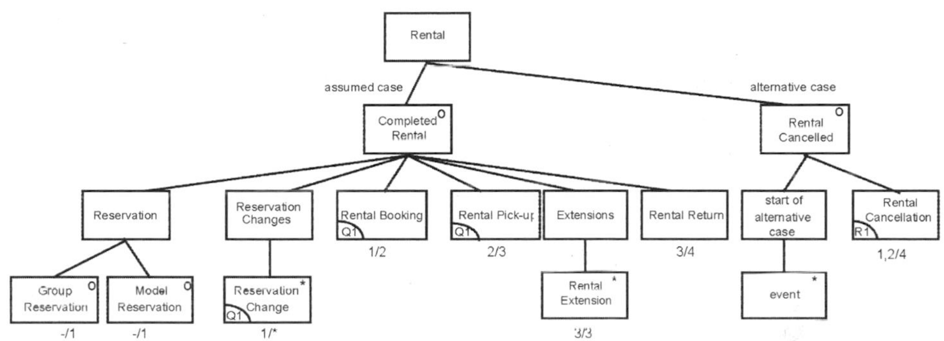

Figure 2-18 Rental Entity Life History with several quit points

A quit label ('Qn') means that, instead of the labelled event's occurring, the corresponding resume ('Rn') event can legitimately occur. In the example above, after creation of a Rental with a Group Reservation or a Model Reservation, a Rental Cancellation might occur:

- instead of a Reservation Change;
- after some Reservation Changes, instead of a Rental Booking;
- after a Rental Booking, instead of a Rental Pick-up.

Once the car has been picked up, the Rental cannot be cancelled.

The set of valid prior state indicator values for the effect annotated with an 'R' is an aggregate of all the sets of valid prior state indicator values for the corresponding effects annotated with a 'Q'.

Operations

An operation is a discrete unit of logical processing which, either singularly or in combination with others, constitutes an event's effect, and if thought useful can be added to the Entity Life History diagram.

Operations can be useful in discovering overlooked events within Entity Life History analysis by asking pertinent questions such as:

- when is this calculation performed?
- when is this attribute value updated?
- when is this attribute value deleted?

All operations are uniquely identified throughout the whole system (although unique identifiers can be used on individual diagrams as illustrated in the examples in this chapter). Operation identifiers are shown on the diagram in small boxes attached beneath the effect to which they relate. An effect may be the result of more than one operation. An effect may have no explicit operations during Entity Life History analysis where the event simply changes the state of the entity.

If possible, operations should be added to effect boxes in the sequence they will be executed.

Operations should be expressed in a structured format to give a clear specification to designers and implementers. If the target technology type is known at the time of developing operation definitions, the syntax of operations can be chosen to be consistent with the types of procedures that will be used to implement the system.

The set of logical operations used in Entity Life Histories should cover the types that are listed below. The operation types listed can be used as a default set if the implementation environment is not known at the point of developing operation specifications.

Operation type	Logical Processing Description
Create <entity>	This will apply to a birth effect. Values of the primary key of the entity and mandatory attributes will be set to values input with the event that creates the entity. For optional attributes, if values are not provided with the event, default values are set, or values are assumed to be 'null'. May be modified by a 'set' operation (see below).
Set <attribute>	Alter the value held within the attribute to the new value input with the event.
Set <attribute> using <expression>	Alter the value held within the attribute to the result of the value in the expression; this can be used to supplement a 'create' operation if attributes will be set to values distinct from input values.
Tie to <entity>	Establish a relationship between this entity and a master entity.
Cut from <entity>	Remove the relationship between this entity and a master entity.
Gain <entity>	Establish a relationship between this entity and a detail entity.
Lose <entity>	Remove the relationship between this entity and a detail entity.
Swap <entity>	Swap relationships from one occurrence of a master entity to another occurrence of the same master entity.
Invoke <process>	Invoke the process known as <process> which is defined elsewhere, possibly as a super-event or common enquiry.

The 'Create' and 'Set' operations are the main types that are added to the Entity Life History.

The 'Gain' and 'Lose' operations are only significant as a validation aid to the practitioner within Entity Life History analysis and may be omitted if they are found to be unhelpful. Where they are used on Entity Life Histories, 'Gain' and 'Lose' operations can be used to check the following:

- for each 'Gain' operation on a master entity there should be a 'Tie' operation on the detail entity which corresponds;
- for each 'Lose' operation on a master entity there should be a 'Cut' operation on the detail entity which corresponds.

Where there is more than one 'valid previous' value of the state indicator for a particular effect, it is possible to have conditions attached to operations under that effect which test for the value of the state indicator and execute particular operations only if the state indicator is of a particular value (or within a range of values). In this case, an operation can be preceded by the phrase 'If SI = <value> ...'.

The following types of operation should not be identified on the Entity Life History diagram:

- accessing entity for database navigation purposes;
- deletion;
- data validation;
- manipulating/sorting data items prior to writing;
- reading an entity prior to updating it.

These types of operation will be dealt with during production of the Effect Correspondence Diagrams and Update Process Models during Conceptual Process Modelling (see Chapter 3).

An example Entity Life History with operations added is shown in Figure 2-19.

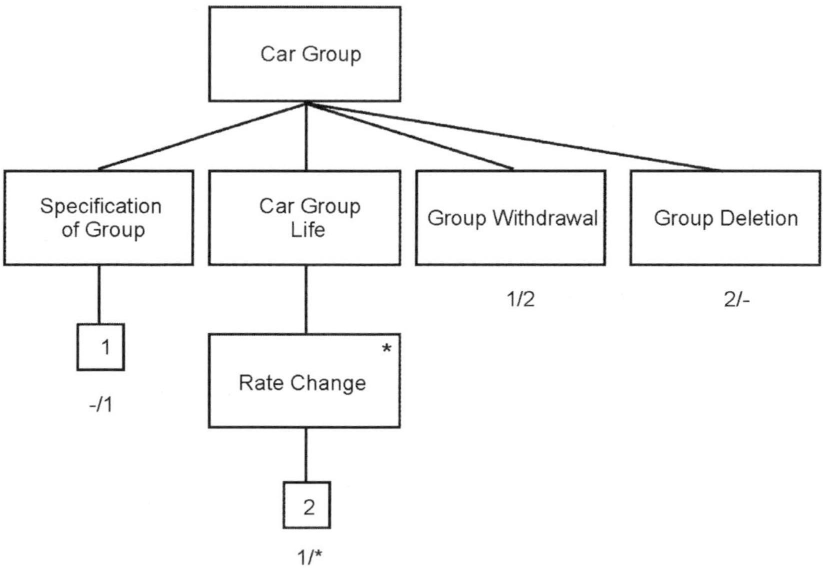

Figure 2-19 Entity Life History of Car Group with operations

Super-events

Super-events are identified on Entity Life Histories for two reasons:

- to simplify Entity Life History diagrams by reducing the number of boxes;
- to help to identify common processing.

A super-event is recognised when two or more events are seen to have exactly the same effect (in terms of operations) on an entity at the same point in its life. Where the same set of events acts in the same way in the life of another entity, the super-event name can be used instead of the individual event names. This type of situation is normally encountered where there is a hierarchy on a Logical Data Structure and sets of events cascade in the same way down the hierarchy. For example, in the EU-Rent system, there is a hierarchy of Car Group, Car Model and Car on the Logical Data Structure as shown in Figure 2-20.

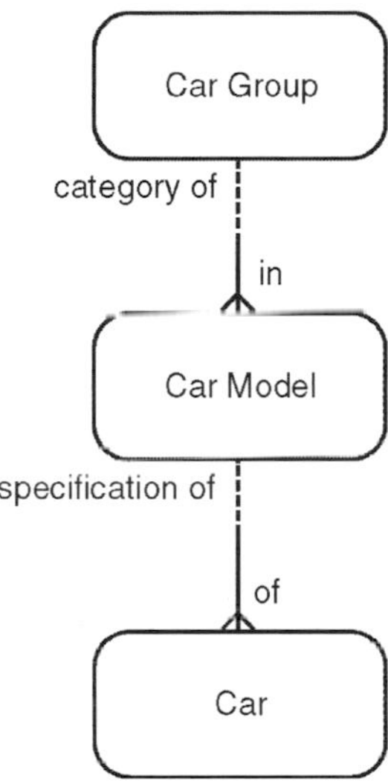

Figure 2-20 Logical Data Structure extract

The removal of a Car Group will cause the death of Car Models within the group and Cars within the model within the group. It is also possible to remove a Car Model without affecting Car Group. This, too, will cause the death of Car. On the Entity Life Histories, therefore, we have the situation shown in Figure 2-21.

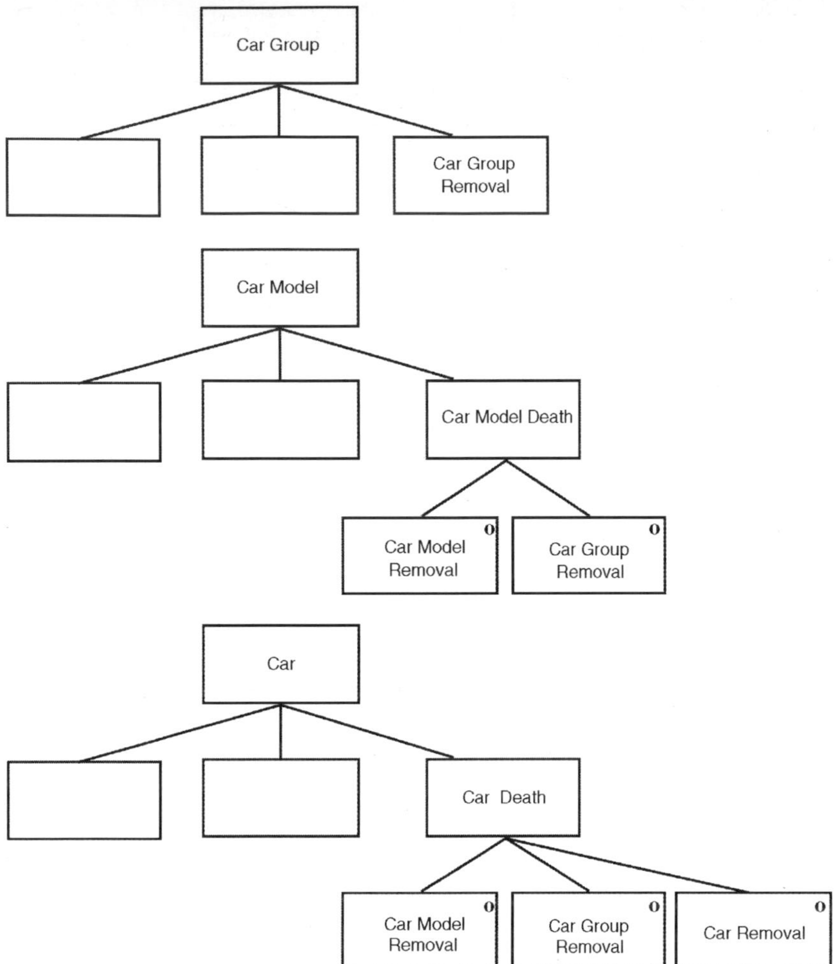

Figure 2-21 Cascading events

In these partial Entity Life Histories, it can be seen that the death events for Car Model will have equivalent effects. In the Car Entity Life History, Car Model Removal and Car Group Removal also have the same effects. Therefore, it is possible to make Car Model Removal and Car Group Removal into a super-event of 'Car Model Death' and refer to the super event in the Car Entity Life History. This is shown in Figure 2-22.

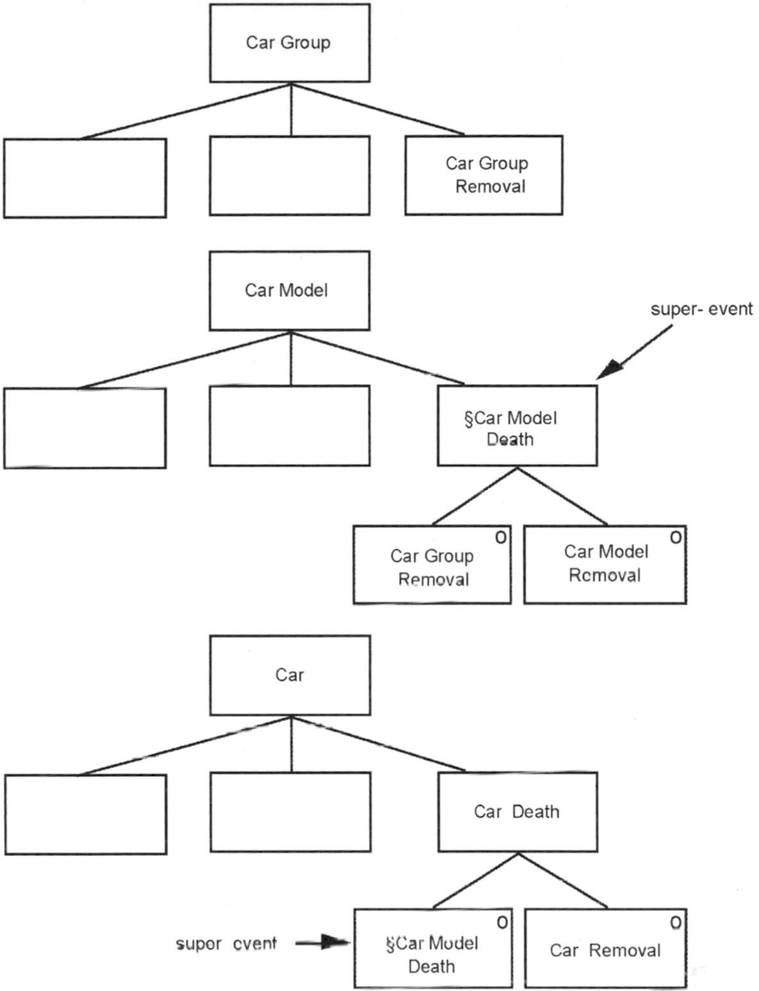

Figure 2-22 Super-events on Entity Life Histories

There are several things to note about the usc of super-events in this example:

- the super-event is annotated with a '§' to denote that it is a super-event (any special character could be used for this purpose);
- the event Car Group Removal still exists in its own right on the Car Group Entity Life History.

Super-events are documented in the Event and Enquiry Catalogue. They can be separately identified on the Entity Access Matrix in addition to the events covered by the super-events.

2.3 Entity Behaviour Modelling Technique

The activities of Enquiry Identification, Event Identification and Entity Life History Analysis are as follows:

- identify enquiries;
- identify events;
- document enquiries and events;
- develop Entity Life Histories.

In practice, these activities will overlap and interact as represented in Figure 2-23.

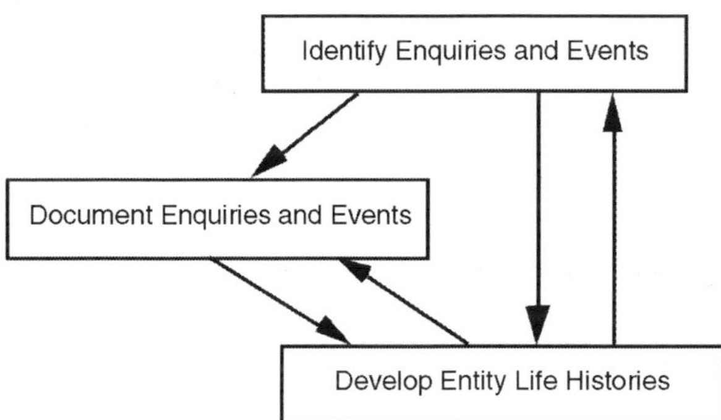

Figure 2-23 Activities of Entity Behaviour Modelling

Event and enquiry identification will be the first activities to be started, but as Entity Life Histories are developed, more events may be identified which means that the documentation of events needs to be updated, having a knock-on effect to Entity Life Histories and so on.

These activities are described in more detail in the following paragraphs.

2.3.1 Identify Enquiries

The identification of enquiries is done by considering the requirements for information support to business activities. These requirements are documented in the Requirements Catalogue and can be checked in consultation with the user.

Requirements for enquiries are derived by examining the information support requirements for the business activities. This will be primarily documented in the Requirements Catalogue. These entries should be supplemented with detailed discussion with the users about the enquiry requirements. Each enquiry can be used to check that the Logical Data Model is able to provide the data to satisfy that enquiry. As the Logical Data Model is validated against enquiries:

- create a row in the Entity Access Matrix for each enquiry and mark each entity accessed;
- identify the attributes needed for each entity to support the enquiry and add them to the Enquiry Description.

If different Business System Options (see the *SSADM Foundation* volume in this series) include different subsets of functional requirements from the Requirements Catalogue, it may be necessary to create several sub-views of the Entity Access Matrix to reflect the fact that not all enquiries are included in each option.

2.3.2 Identify Events

Once the Required System Data Flow Model has been developed, it may be possible to identify events by considering the updates to main data stores. The identification of events can also be done by considering the entities on the Logical Data Model and determining the events that will cause their insertion, modification and deletion. The development of Entity Life Histories will also identify additional events.

There should be a correlation between events and business events documented as part of the Business Activity Model (see *The Business Context* volume in this series). In many cases, business events may be the starting point for identifying events. Where possible, event names should be chosen which correspond to business event names.

As events are identified, they are added to the Entity Access Matrix and documented using the Event and Enquiry Catalogue.

The identification of events is described under the following headings:

- Identifying events from the Required System Data Flow Model and functions;
- Identifying changes which result from events.

Identifying events from the Required System Data Flow Model and functions

The External Design is based on functions which effectively package up events and enquiries for the user. It is therefore useful to check the specification of the External Design to identify events. By checking functions against events and enquiries, it is possible to ensure that each function is associated with at least one event and/or enquiry and each event and enquiry is associated with at least one function.

In the same way that it is possible to identify functions from the Required System Data Flow Model, it is also possible to identify some events from the Required System Data Flow Model.

An extract from the Required System Data Flow Model is shown in Figure 2-24.

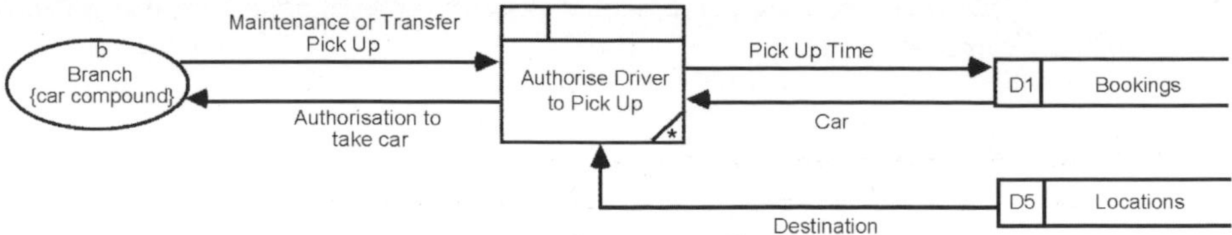

Figure 2-24 Extract from Required System Data Flow Diagrams

This extract in total identifies the function 'Driver Authorisation'. However, this is an update function and is user-initiated, so it must represent at least one event. The event(s) will be notified by the user and the effects of the event(s) can be deduced from the fact that a data store is being updated. By tracing the input from the user through to the update, the event 'Pick-up authorised' is identified.

Events and enquiries can be identified in parallel with functions. As each function is identified, the corresponding events and enquires should also be identified and added to the Entity Access Matrix and Event and Enquiry Catalogue.

Identifying changes which result from events

Where attributes have been defined for a Logical Data Model, it is possible to identify the changes that are needed to keep the values of the data up-to-date. From the changes that are needed, we can look for the business events that originate the changes. From the business events it is possible to identify the events which will cause the system processes to alter the stored data. It is these events that are documented on the Entity Access Matrix.

Once events have been identified, they are added to the Entity Access Matrix and the type of action associated with the effects of the events on the entities added to the intersections. Also, entries are made in the Event and Enquiry Catalogue.

Every entity from the Logical Data Model should be examined for requirements to make the following types of change within the boundary of the system under investigation:

- **Birth** – Each entity on the Entity Access Matrix should be associated with at least one event that causes its creation (insertion). In the example Entity Access Matrix shown in Figure 2-2, these are marked as 'I';
- **Death** – Each entity may be associated with one or more events that causes its death. In this context, death means that the entity is no longer active within the system and is not necessarily synonymous with deletion. For a death effect, the intersection of the Entity Access Matrix is marked with a 'D';
- **changing relationships with masters** – Where an entity has one or more relationships with masters on the Logical Data Model, it is useful to consider what may cause these relationships to be created, changed or severed. Many of these changes to relationships will be associated with birth or death, but a number of other events may be identified which change the relationships. Where a relationship is created, the Entity Access Matrix can be annotated with a 'T' (tie) and corresponding 'G' (gain); and where a relationship is severed, the Entity Access

Matrix can be annotated with a 'C' (cut) and corresponding 'L' (lose). An 'S' (swap masters) and a corresponding 'X' (swap from detail) indicate where a relationship is swapped from one occurrence of a master to another;

- **changing relationships with details** – 'Gains' and 'Losses' are added to the Entity Access Matrix at the intersection between the event and the associated masters. Where a 'G' is marked against an entity, it is this entity that will be gaining a detail. 'L' (lose) can be used on the Entity Access Matrix to denote the severance of a relationship from master to detail and 'X' can be used to denote the swapping of a relationship from one occurrence of a detail to another;

- **changing values of non-key attributes** – Identify the events which cause attributes (other than primary and foreign keys) to be updated. Any attributes that are mandatory will have a value assigned at the birth of the entity but it is possible that their value can be altered by events during the life of the entity in the system. Attributes that are optional may not need to have a value assigned at the birth of the entity and may indicate events that add values and change values or remove values during the life of the entity in the system;

- **state-changing event(s) and date-driven event(s)** – An event may change the state of an entity without necessarily affecting any other attributes or relationships. It usually 'freezes' or 'thaws' the entity in some way. To 'freeze' an entity is to move it into a state where some types of event are no longer permitted to affect it. To 'thaw' it is to move it into a state where the events are again permitted. This is one way of enforcing business rules.

By considering these types of requirement, it should be possible to identify events. Care should be taken to ensure that where the same event is identified in the context of several different entities, it is identified as the same event and documented only once.

Note that the behaviour of entities within a system may need to be co-ordinated with the behaviour of entities in other systems. For example, some entities may be created or deleted by other systems outside the boundary set for a particular project.

2.3.3 Document Enquiries and Events

Events and enquiries are documented in the Event and Enquiry Catalogue.

In analysing the Logical Data Model we identify the changes that are required to update the system data. To complete the matrix, we also have to;

- name the events in terms that are meaningful to users, preferably with reference to business events

  For example, in EU-Rent what business event causes swap of Car from one branch's Car Stock to another (modelling change of ownership of a car from one branch to another)? Is it Transfer Booking, Transfer Pick-up, or Transfer Drop-off? When the users are consulted, they confirm that it is Transfer Pick-up. It is this business event that is used as the event.

- look for multiple events that have the same effects on entities

  For example, in EU-Rent, is Transfer Pick-up the only event that can cause change of ownership of a car between branches? A one-way rental can also cause change of ownership. The swap occurs when the car is dropped off at the destination branch. Is Rental Drop-off a reasonable name for the event? As it turns out, EU-Rent users refer to 'Rental Return', even when the car is not returned to the branch from which it was rented.

- define the correspondence between functions and events as all events will be notified through functions. This is done to ensure that:
  - every event is notified to the system as input to at least one function;
  - events have been identified to make the changes required by every update function.

2.3.4 Develop Entity Life Histories

Entity Life Histories are developed from information taken from the Entity Access Matrix, adding in the constraints and sequencing that need to be considered for the system under development. The development of Entity Life Histories can help to validate the Logical Data Model and may identify events that have been missed.

Entity Life Histories can be developed through a number of steps. These steps arrange knowledge acquisition into a reasonably natural sequence of questions and answers, developing from a simple picture towards the full detail required for implementation of the system.

In general, it is useful to start at the bottom of the Logical Data Model and work upwards in drafting of Entity Life Histories as this allows the analyst to identify any interdependencies between the lives of detail and master.

The steps in developing Entity Life Histories are as follows:

- Analysis and specification of basic behaviour;
- 'Up-pass' analysis of behaviour;
- 'Down-pass' analysis of behaviour;
- Analysis and specification of deletion strategy (if this is being included);
- Addition of operations and state indicators (if being used).

These steps are described in more detail in the following paragraphs and their use demonstrated by examples from the EU-Rent case study.

Analysis and specification of basic behaviour

The events which have an updating or state changing effect on the entity are extracted from the Entity Access Matrix as a starting point. The matrix indicates whether the effects create, amend or kill the entity, so there will be an initial indication of where in the life the effects should be placed.

The following activities are undertaken:

- **Identify major state changes**. Identify events which will move the entity into a new phase of its life. The phases should relate to business constraints such that each new state will be recognised by the user and will constrain other events that are allowed to occur. For example, in some systems, an 'authorisation' event is often required to move an entity from an unauthorised state to an authorised state after which fewer amendments are permitted. Death effects will also cause major state changes. Arrange the major state change effects in sequence;
- **Identify effects of events permitted between major state changes**. Identify events that trigger elementary update effects on the entity. Examine the sequence of major state changes and identify which elementary update effects are permitted in each major state. For example, amendments to attributes are often permitted during the life of an entity but not after its 'death';
- **Draw simple Entity Life History**. Record only valid sequences of events in a life. Working from the bottom of the data model to the top, for each entity, show:
  - birth before death;
  - major state changes in a left-to-right sequence between the birth and death interspersed with the elementary update effects.
- **Identify events with more than one effect on an entity**. Distinguish between two or more effects of an event on one entity. Decide whether the effects are alternatives for one another for the same entity occurrences or whether the event is affecting different occurrences of the entity in different roles (simultaneously). Effect Qualifiers are used to distinguish alternative effects and entity role are used to denote simultaneous effects.

From the EU-Rent system, the entity Rental has the following events cross referenced:

- Walk-in Rental;
- Reservation;
- Reservation Change;
- Rental Booking;
- Rental Pick-up;
- Rental Extension;
- Rental Return.

Firstly, the events are examined to find out which ones are likely to represent the major milestones in the life of the entity and affect what else can be done to the entity. For example, from the list above, it can be seen that the event Walk-in Rental and Reservation will start the life of Rental and the event Rental Return will be near the end of its life. Rental Booking is likely to be a major event – after this has affected Rental, the car may be written off. Also, the event Rental Pick-up will have a major effect – after this has affected Rental, there can be no more rescheduling but extensions to the Rental may be required.

Next, events are identified which can affect the entity before or after the events which represent the milestones in the entity's life and arranged into a rough sequence. From the list above, the event Reservation Change can only affect the Rental entity before Rental Booking affects the entity and the event Rental Extension can only happen after the Rental Pick-up.

Having identified the events and placed them in a rough sequence, it is possible to draw an initial Entity Life History for the entity. The first attempt at the Entity Life History for the entity Rental is shown in Figure 2-25.

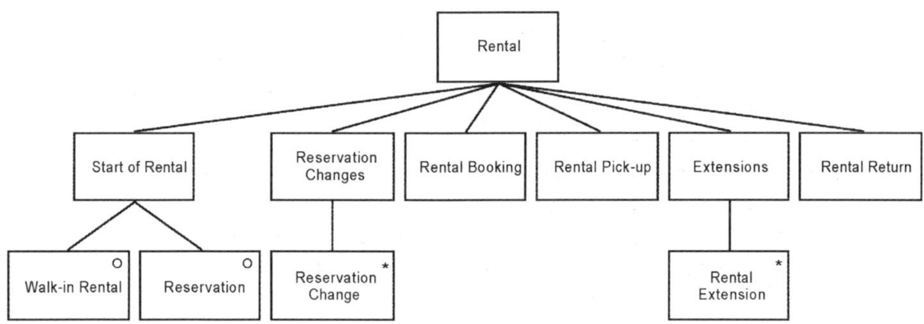

Figure 2-25 First attempt at Entity Life History for Rental

Where an event has two or more effects in one life it can be placed in several different places in the Entity Life History. Whenever the same event appears more than once in an Entity Life History, each of its different effects must be distinguished using an effect qualifier or entity role name. For example, in the Rental Entity Life History, the event Rental Return has two different effects on the entity depending on whether the car is dropped of at the depot it was rented from or at some other depot. This is represented in Figure 2-26.

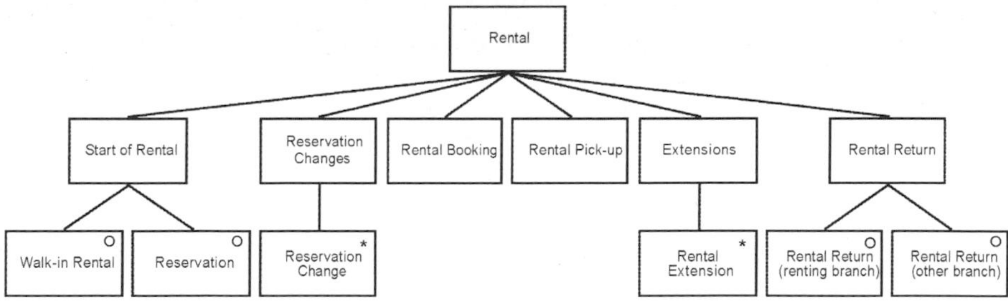

Figure 2-26 Two different effects of Rental Return shown on ELH

'Up-pass' analysis of behaviour

Working from the bottom of the data model to the top, follow this guidance for each entity:

- **Separate parallel aspects**. If there is a clash between patterns of events, either use the parallel structure notation or, for more complex parallel lives, split the original entity into aspects. Assign each attribute and relationship of the entity to one of the aspects. Draw an Entity Life History for each aspect. Entity Aspects are explained more fully in the *Data Modelling* volume in this series.
- **Analyse and specify mutually exclusive behaviour patterns**. For alternative cases use a selection to specify the different patterns of events and use the quit and resume convention where necessary. For sub/super-types draw two Entity Life Histories: one for the super-type and one which contains a selection, each option of which is the life of one of the sub-types.
- **Analyse and specify cyclical behaviour patterns**. Look for sequences of events in any iterated selection of events. If there are other events in the iterated selection that are not included in the sequence, separate them from events in the cycle, by creating a parallel life. Consider the birth and death of details of this entity. Decide whether the birth and death of a detail should be included in the life of the master either to constrain the life or to change attributes in the master. The inclusion of birth and death of details is likely to be represented as a repeated sequence at a particular point in the life of the master.
- **Identify how a cyclical behaviour stops**. For each cyclical behaviour pattern, specify how the cyclical behaviour pattern ends, whether in a controlled or random way. Some entities will be constrained to die after a specific point in their lives, controlled by the user. Others will die at any point in their life, based on the notification of a business event which is outside the control of the user.
- **See if new detail entities are needed**. Given an iterated event that is not already the birth or death of a detail entity, imagine the event as the birth of a new detail entity, and decide whether it would be useful to add a new detail entity under this master on the Logical Data Model.

This can be demonstrated by looking at the Entity Life History for the Rental entity from EU-Rent – it is apparent that Walk-in Rentals may be substantially different from those that are reserved in advance. To test out whether the lives are different from beginning to end, a high-level selection is introduced into the Entity Life History and each life is looked at in isolation as shown in Figure 2-27. This is a useful way of sorting out potentially complicated Entity Life Histories. Instead of trying to cover all situations at once, it helps to draw separate lives for different scenarios before trying to merge them into a single life.

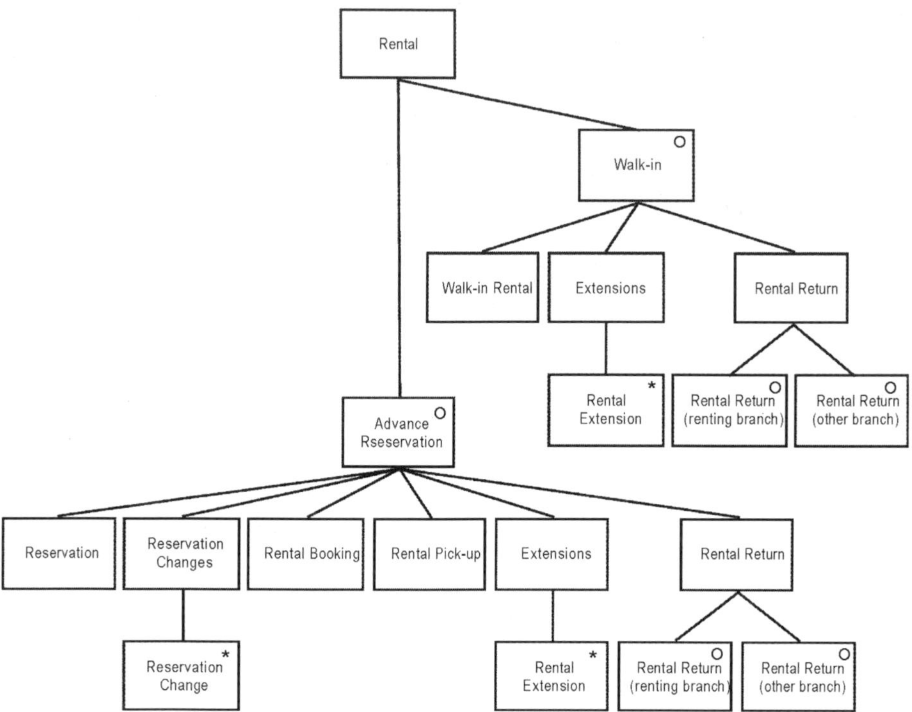

Figure 2-27 Separate lives for walk-in and advance reservation rentals

By comparing the two different lives for Rental, it can be seen that there is a lot of commonality in the back-end of the Rental. Each Rental may start in a slightly different way, but once a car is driven away, they behave in exactly the same way. The Entity Life History for Rental is modified to show this (see Figure 2-28).

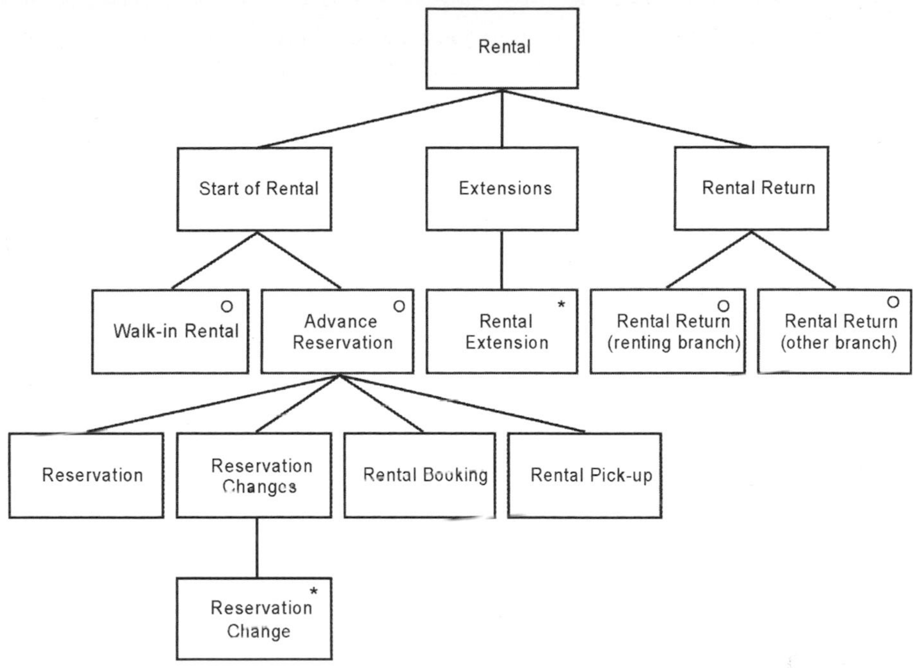

Figure 2-28 Rental Entity Life History with common parts of different lives

Entity Life Histories can be developed further by looking for sequences of events under iterated selections, identifying how iterations are terminated, and checking relationships with connected entities.

Down-pass analysis of behaviour

Working from the top of the Logical Data Model to the bottom, analyse each master-detail pair. The following guidelines should be used.

- **Identify extra death events**. For each entity, list any further potential death events that have not so far been considered. Name any events specific to the entity (such as real-world death, damage or re-classification) that can cause its life to be cut short;
- **Specify 'cascade' effects of death event**. Where the relationship from detail to master is mandatory, the master's death event will often kill off its currently active detail entities. If this is true, the master's death event should be included as a death event in the life of the details;
- **Specify 'restricted' effects of death event**. In some cases the master's death is only allowed after all details have died. In this case, it is possible to indicate this by putting the death of the detail as an effect in the master's life to indicate this restriction. Alternatively, an operation can be added under the death event in the master's life which tests the pre-condition that all details should be dead in order that this effect is allowed to continue;

- **Specify 'set null' or 'swap master' effects of death event**. If the master's death event cuts its relationship to a detail (or swaps the detail entity to another master) then the detail entity may live on after the master's death, and so the master's death event should be added somewhere in the middle of the detail entity's life;
- **Include detail's extra death events in master's life**. For each entity with more than one master, consideration should be given to including the birth and death events of the detail entity in the master's Entity Life History;
- **Identify Super-events**. Look for similar patterns of effects in different Entity Life Histories. Where two or more events have exactly the same effect at the same point in a life, they can be combined into a super-event. Wherever the same combination of events occurs in other Entity Life Histories, the super-event name can be used provided that the effects are identical. Super-events are likely to be identified where there are cascading deaths.

The death/deletion of connected entities will be determined to some extent by the type of relationship connecting them so the approach to finding out how the death of one entity affects another centres on the rules for deleting relationships. The three broad categories that should be considered are:

- cascade, where the death of the master is also the death of the detail;
- restrict, where the death of the master is restricted by the death of the detail;
- orphan/swap, where the death of the master causes the detail to become detached or swapped to another master.

Cascade death

Where the relationship from detail to master is mandatory, the master's death event will often kill off its currently active detail entities. If this is true, the event causing the death of the master's should be included in the life of the details.

With a **Shared Death** a detail entity dies when its master dies, and has no separate death defined as illustrated in Figure 2-29.

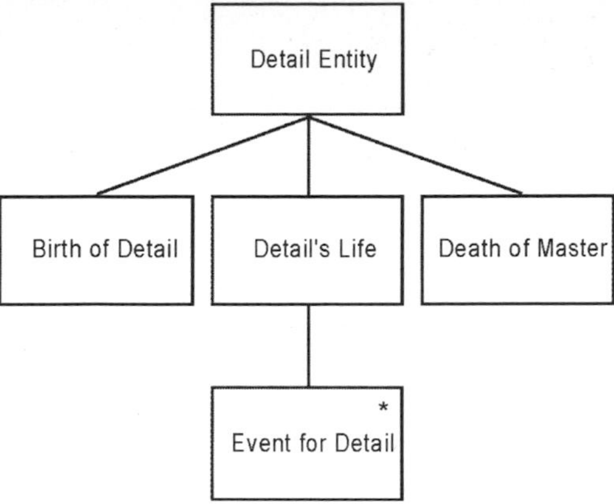

Figure 2-29 Shared death

An example of this from EU-Rent is that all Rentals could potentially be held on the system until Customer is removed. When Customer is removed, all Rentals belonging to that customer would be removed as well.

With an **Alternate death** a detail entity is killed either when its specific death event occurs or when its master's death occurs, whichever happens first. This is illustrated in Figure 2-30.

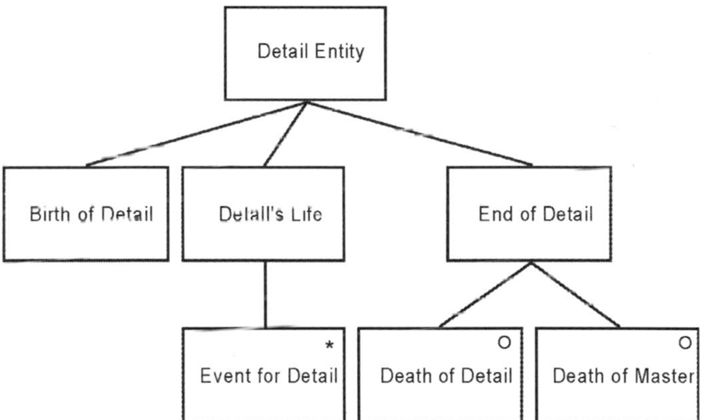

Figure 2-30 Alternate death

For example, from EU-Rent, it is possible that a decision could be made that Car Transfers are retained for one year or until Branch Closure, whichever came first.

Restricted Death

In some cases the master's death is only allowed after all details have died. There are two possibilities, the 'controlled death' and the 'intended death'.

In the **controlled death** model, the master's death is not allowed to happen if it has any live details.

There are two approaches that can be used here. First, if 'dead' details are to be retained as history until the master's death, upon which the details are deleted, the 'shared death' model (described above) can be used for the detail as shown in Figure 2-31. Note, this shows that details are retained until the master dies. The event Death of Master deletes the detail entity.

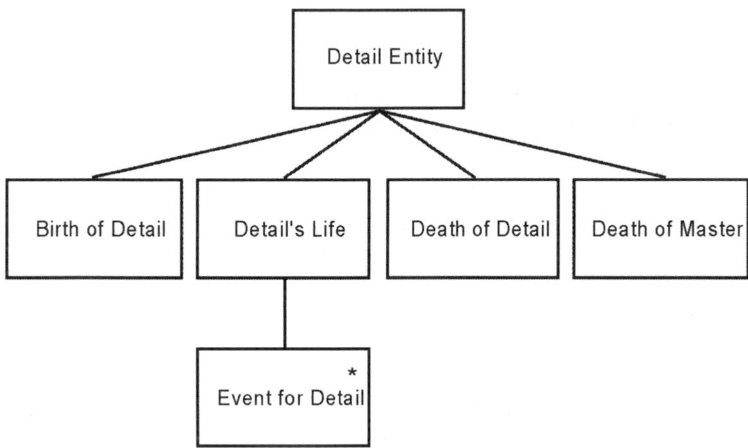

Figure 2-31 Use of 'shared death' in detail ELH to control death of master

As well as showing that the event Death of Master deletes the detail entity, it also shows the constraint that if there are any occurrences of the detail for which 'Death of Detail' has not occurred, then the event 'Death of Master' cannot proceed: the master cannot die until all of its details are dead.

If details are actually removed before the master and not retained, it is necessary to include a 'fail' operation in the master's life which prevents the death if any details still exist. This is illustrated in Figure 2-32.

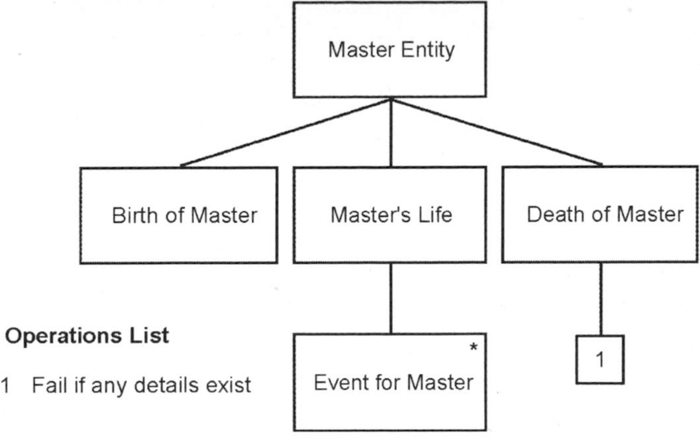

Figure 2-32 Use of operation to impose controlled death

In the **Intended death** model, a master can be put into a state whereby it will be automatically removed when all of its details are gone. The death of the last detail is the death of the master. This is illustrated in Figure 2-33.

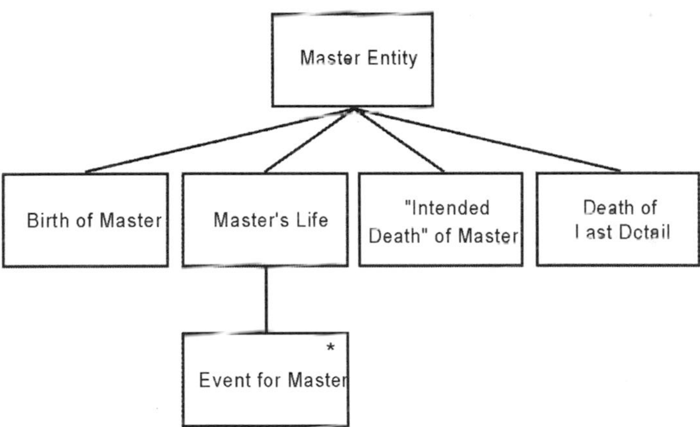

Figure 2-33 Intended death

For example, in EU-Rent, when the decision is taken to close a branch (the 'intended death'), it cannot actually be closed until all of its cars have been sold, written-off or transferred to other branches. It can be removed when the last car goes.

Orphan/Swap

If the master's death event cuts its relationship to a detail (or swaps the detail entity to another master) then the detail entity may live on after the master's death, and so the master's death event should be added somewhere in the middle of the detail entity's life. This is illustrated in Figure 2-34.

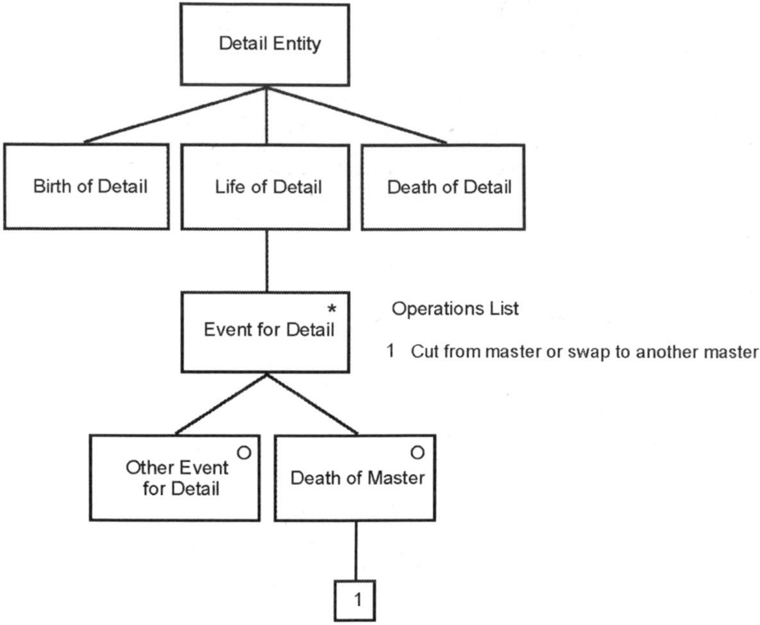

Figure 2-34 Death of master shown in life of detail

For example, in EU-Rent, the event Car Write-off may affect Rental, but does not remove it, as shown in the Rental Entity Life History in Figure 2-35. In this diagram, the death of Car is shown under the life of Rental. The loss of the car does not affect the Rental in any way other than another car must be found before the car is picked up by the customer.

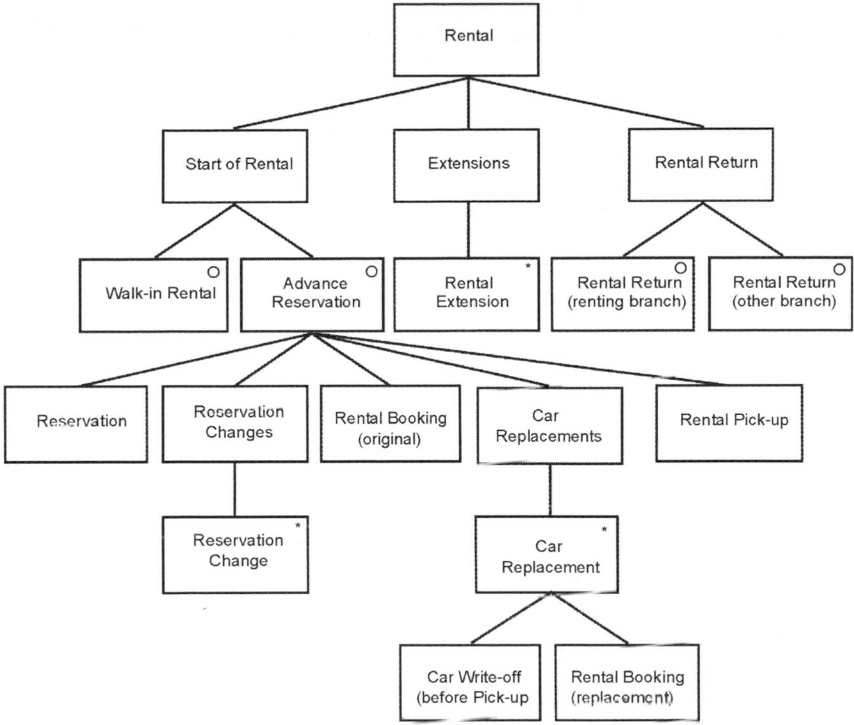

Figure 2-35 Death of master (Car) in life of Rental

Analysis & specification of deletion strategy (if being examined)

The death of entities has been considered as being when the entities are no longer able to play an active role within the system. The actual point at which entity occurrences are removed from the live data may be at this point or at a later point, depending upon the deletion and archive strategy.

The following guidelines should be followed:

- **Specify deletion events**. If an entity need not be retained for enquiries on historical information, then death may be considered synonymous with deletion and the state indicator set to null. If historical information must be retained after death, the subsequent deletion effect should be identified (sometimes this is the deletion of a master). Specify any events that may affect the entity between death and deletion and add them to the Entity Life History;

- **Analyse & specify reversions**. A reversion causes the entity to return to an earlier state in its life, for example if a bank account is closed down, a reversion would be an event which causes the account to be re-opened. For each major state change in the Entity Life History, there may be a requirement to allow a reversion in certain circumstances. For every possible reversion there is usually an alternative effect which confirms that the normal sequence of events will take place. In the bank account example, a confirmation would be that the account is deleted, preventing the reversion from taking place. In the lives of connected entities, consider replacing the event before the reversion with the confirmation event.

Add operations and state indicators

- **Add operations to effects on the structure**. Operations to maintain attributes and relationships should be added to the relevant effects on the Entity Life History diagram;
- **Add State Indicators to the structure**. Add 'valid previous' and 'set to' state indicator values to each effect on the Entity Life History Diagram. Optimise state indicator values set by selections and iterations where required. Where an entity has only two states (null and '1') there is no need to add state indicators to the diagram.

2.4 Relationship with other analysis and design techniques

2.4.1 Business Activity Modelling (covered in The Business Context *volume)*

The Business Activity Model contains a definition of business events. From these definitions, the set of events that will trigger processes in the Conceptual Model can be derived.

2.4.2 Function Definition (covered the Function Modelling *and* User Centred Design volumes*)*

Function Definition helps to identify events and enquiries and group them within functions.

An event/enquiry may be input via more than one function and so be referenced by several Function Descriptions. For each function the analyst must check to see that the attributes for the event/enquiry are contained in the input to or can be generated by the function.

After consultation with the user, output from the Entity Behaviour Modelling technique will be used to update the Function Definition products by:

- adding newly identified events and enquiries to existing functions;
- identifying the need for new functions.

Consistency checks are required to ensure that all events and enquiries are assigned to the appropriate functions. In most cases assignment will be on a 1-1 basis but where more complex relationships exist between events and functions a function/event matrix could be used to help in providing quality consistency.

2.4.3 *Logical Data Modelling (covered in the* Data Modelling *volumes)*

The Required System Logical Data Model contains the entities upon which Entity Life Histories are based and is used to create the Entity Access Matrix in the first instance.

Enquiries are a powerful tool in the development and validation of the Logical Data Model.

The detailed data analysis in the Entity Life History technique is likely to improve the practitioner's understanding of the entities in the system and may lead to substantial changes being made to the Logical Data Model.

2.4.4 *Conceptual Process Modelling (covered in Chapter 3)*

Conceptual Process Modelling products are derived directly from Entity Behaviour Modelling products. Effect Correspondence Diagrams are derived from the Entity Life Histories and Entity Access Matrix. Enquiry Access Paths are drawn for each of the enquiries identified.

3 CONCEPTUAL PROCESS MODELLING

Conceptual Process Modelling defines the processing required in response to events or enquiries. Conceptual Process Modelling covers a set of techniques which model the accessing of the Required System Logical Data Model by events and enquiries and the operations required to support the processing of the events and enquiries.

There are four techniques for Conceptual Process Modelling;

- Enquiry Access Paths;
- Effect Correspondence Diagrams;
- Enquiry Process Models;
- Update Process Models.

These are shown in the context of the System Development Template in Figure 3-1 below.

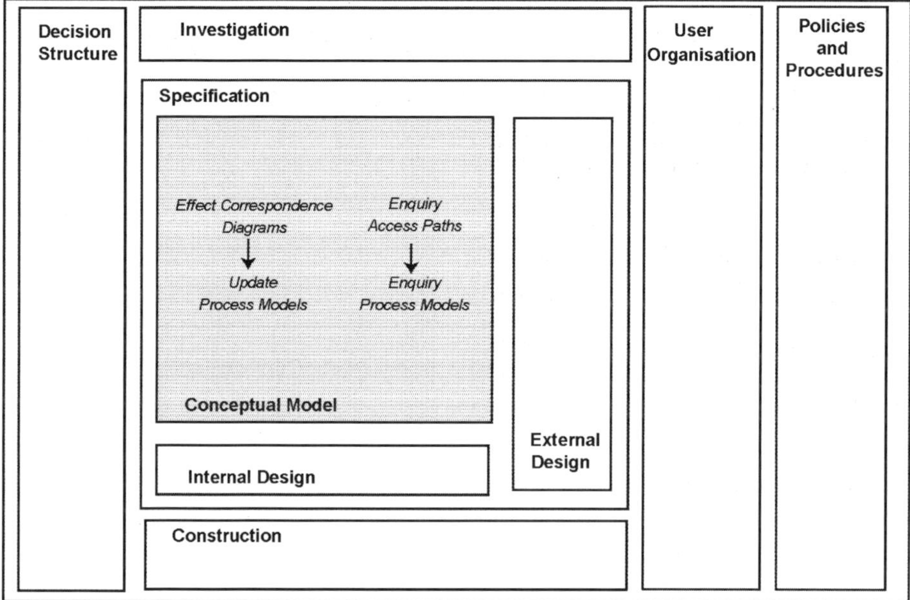

Figure 3-1 Conceptual Process Modelling in the System Development Template

The purposes of each of the individual techniques are described as follows:

- **Enquiry Access Paths** serve several purposes:
  - validating the Required System Logical Data Model by testing it against requirements for information support to the business;

  - specifying enquiries in an unambiguous way;
  - creating structures for enquiry processes.

- **Effect Correspondence Diagrams** provide structures for update processes;
- **Enquiry Process Models** transform Enquiry Access Paths into Jackson-like structures which present the enquiry processes in a format that will provide a route through into physical design for certain types of environment;
- **Update Process Models** transform Effect Correspondence Diagrams into Jackson-like structures which present the update processes in a format that will provide a route through into physical design for certain types of environment.

Effect Correspondence Diagrams and Enquiry Access Paths are the specification of the processing required to support events and enquiries. Almost all of what is in an Effect Correspondence Diagram is derived from the Entity Access Matrix, the Entity Life Histories (ELH) and the Required System Logical Date Model[1]:

- what entities are affected by each event, and whether there are multiple effects;
- where there are multiple effects, whether they are alternatives for the same occurrences of the entity or simultaneous effects on different instances;
- explicit operations from the ELH and operations implied by the syntax of the ELH;
- what correspondences can be supported.

This information is taken as the starting point for Effect Correspondence Diagrams and developed into a processing specification for each event.

Enquiry Access Paths serve a similar purpose to Effect Correspondence Diagrams. They are derived from the Entity Access Matrix and Required System Logical Data Model. They are developed to support the information needs of the business.

Enquiry Process Models and Update Process Models are transformations of Enquiry Access Paths and Effect Correspondence Diagrams into full Jackson notation.

3.1 Products of Conceptual Process Modelling

Within Conceptual Process Modelling there are four basic products:

- Enquiry Access Paths;
- Effect Correspondence Diagrams;
- Enquiry Process Models;
- Update Process Models.

---

[1] For a description of the Entity Access Matrix and Entity Life Histories see Chapter 2. For a description of the derivation of the Required System Logical Data Model see the *Data Modelling* volume in this series.

3.1.1 Effect Correspondence Diagrams and Enquiry Access Paths

An Effect Correspondence Diagram (ECD) shows the way in which effects for each event are related to one another and demonstrates the navigation around the Required System Logical Data Model required to process the effects. Similarly, Enquiry Access Paths show all the accesses required of entities on the Logical Data Model and the navigation paths required to retrieve the specified data.

For both types of diagram, the entry point into the Logical Data Model is indicated by an arrow which is annotated with the data items that are provided with the event or enquiry in order to identify the correct entity occurrences and to supply values for attributes required for the event or enquiry processes to be completed. Navigation is indicated by a series of arrows between boxes. Each box represents an effect/access or is a node used to indicate selection or iteration. Figure 3-2 shows the structure conventions for Effect Correspondence Diagrams and Enquiry Access Paths.

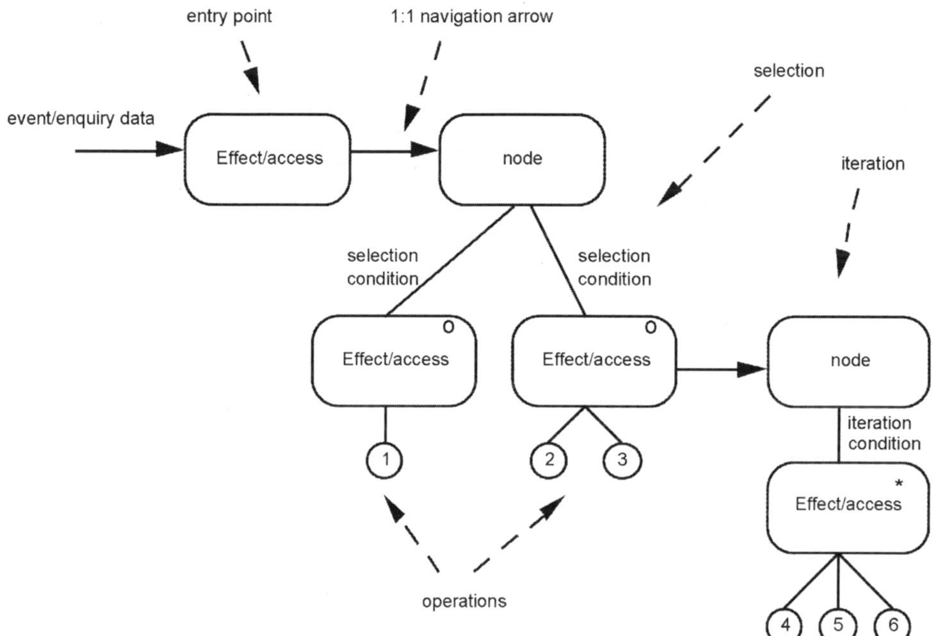

Figure 3-2 Structure Conventions for Enquiry Access Paths and Effect Correspondence Diagrams

All boxes on the diagram are 'soft' boxes. The overall title of the diagram contains the enquiry or event name. The basic structure contains the following components:

- selection represented by a box with two or more boxes below it, each of which contains an 'o' in the top right corner;

- iteration represented by a box with a single box below it containing an asterisk '*' in the top right corner;
- one-to-one navigation arrows between two boxes of any type except the following:
  - between two iterated components (indicated by an asterisk);
  - between two selected components (indicated by an 'o');
  - between a selected component and an iterated component.

An example Enquiry Access Path is shown in Figure 3-3.

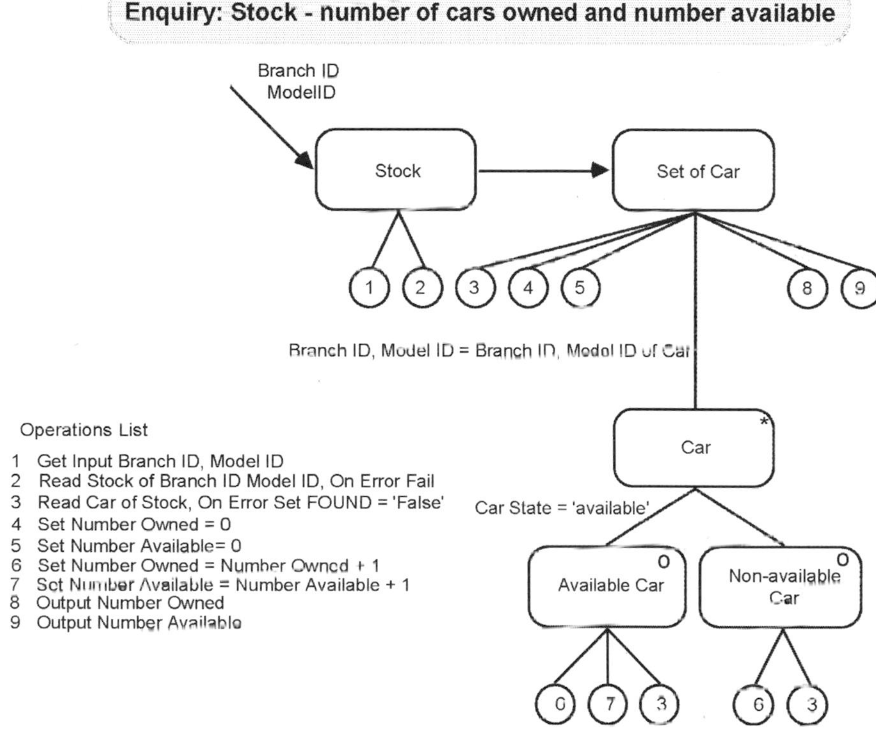

Figure 3-3 Example Enquiry Access Path

Each iteration may be annotated with the condition which determines when the repeating element will be invoked. Conditions used for iterated components can identify sub-sets of iterated components as well as individual components; for example, a condition can be for all occurrences of an entity where the date matches an input date. Each selection may be annotated with the condition which determines when that particular option is selected.

Each effect/access box is given the name of the entity from the Logical Data Model. If an event affects an entity in more than one way, the corresponding number of boxes are added

to the diagram containing the entity name with the effect qualifier or entity role name appended.

Each iteration node is given the name 'Set of <entity name>'. Selection nodes can be named to help describe the choice being made at this point.

The entry point is usually a single effect/access which is identified by primary key. In this case, the attribute(s) of the primary key are annotated on the arrow shown pointing to the box, together with any other data needed to complete the event/enquiry. Where multiple occurrences of the entity used as the entry point need to be accessed, the entry point on the Effect Correspondence Diagram or Enquiry Access Path is shown as an iteration. The entry point can be annotated with data items that will identify a sub-set of the entry point entity occurrences or can be left blank if all occurrences are required.

The operations from the Entity Life Histories, supplemented by further operations, can be attached to the effect/access boxes and the nodes. They are added in the sequence in which they are invoked. Note that the operations that appear on Entity Life Histories and the operations that appear on the Effect Correspondence Diagrams are the same operations (apart from operations that are added to Effect Correspondence Diagrams only). All operations are defined centrally and referenced wherever used. The syntax for operations should be defined by local standards and should, where possible, reflect the physical environment in which the system will be implemeneted.

3.1.2 Enquiry Process Models and Update Process Models

Enquiry and Update Process Models are a transformation of Enquiry Access Paths and Effect Correspondence Diagrams into Jackson-like structures.

The structure conventions for Enquiry and Update Process Models are shown in Figure 3-4.

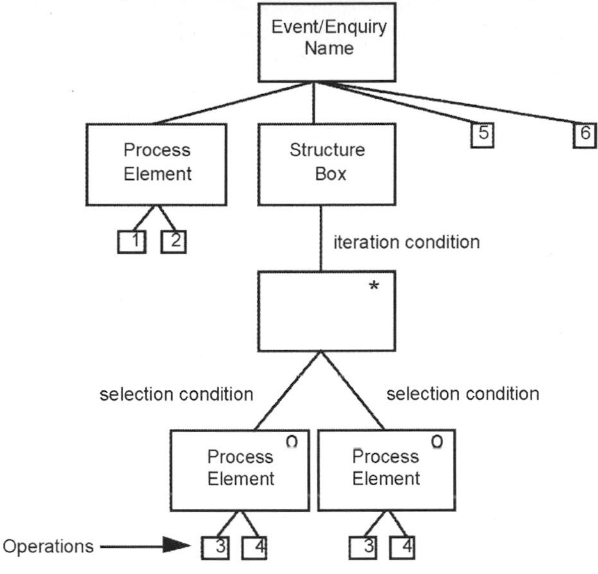

Figure 3-4 Structure conventions for Update and Enquiry Process Models

All boxes on the diagram are 'hard' boxes. The top box of the structure contains the name of the event or enquiry. The structure contains the following components:

- **sequence** represented by a box with a series of plain boxes below it: the plain boxes should be read from left to right;
- **iteration** represented by a box with a single box below it containing an asterisk in the top right corner: the process represented by this box can be repeated a number of times from zero to many;
- **selection** represented by a box with a series of boxes below it containing 'o' in the top right corner: these boxes are alternatives for one another, only one of which will be selected at this point in the structure (if one of the boxes is a 'null' selection, indicated by a dash, then it is possible for none of the alternatives to be selected);

Each bottom leaf on the structure represents the processing of an effect or access from the Effect Correspondence Diagram or Enquiry Access Path.

Some more operations can be added to the boxes on the structure in the sequence in which they are invoked. Operations can be added to structure boxes as well as the 'leaves' of the structure.

Operations are added to the Conceptual Process Modelling products in addition to those which originate in the Entity Life Histories to define the processing more fully. Examples of the types of operation which are added during Conceptual Process Modelling are as follows:

Operation Type	**Logical Processing Description**
Read <entity> by key	Read (from the database) the entity by key using input key value.
Define set of <entity> matching input data	Define a set of <entity> entities, the members of which match the criteria in the input data. This can also be extended to define ordering of items, e.g., 'order by …'.
Read next <entity> in set	Read (from the database) the next entity of type <entity>, from the currently defined set. This operation should always be preceded by a 'Define set' operation.
Read next <detail> of <master> [via <relationship>]	Read (from the database) the next entity of type <detail> related to the current occurrence of <master>. The optional 'via <relationship>' clause is used to identify a particular relationship, where there is more than one relationship between <master> and <detail>.
Read <master> of <detail> [via <relationship>]	Read (from the database) the master of type <master> related to the current occurrence of <detail> using <relationship>. The optional 'via <relationship>' clause is used to identify a particular relationship, where there is more than one relationship between <master> and <detail>.
Fail if <statement>	Abort the entire process if a pre-defined circumstance is met. An actioned fail operation will prevent subsequent operations from being executed.
Fail if state indicator of <entity> outside <value_range>	Raise errors on state indicator outside valid range after reading an entity. Value_range can be a list of values or named states.
Get <data items>	Obtain data items from the function that is invoking the event/enquiry.
Output <data items>	Output data items to the function invoking the event or enquiry.
Set <entity> SI = <value>	Set the value of the state indicator of an entity to a specified value. The value can be numeric or textual.
Write <entity>	Commit all changes to an entity, writing back to the database.
Delete <entity>	Remove entity from the database.

A number of the operation types listed above and in the Entity Behaviour Modelling chapter can be extended to include the phrase 'On Error <action>'. The action would normally set an indicator, fail the process or quit from an iteration to the next part of the process.

The syntax of the operations can be defined locally – the examples above, supplemented with the operations listed in the Entity Behaviour Modelling chapter, are the type of operations that may be required as part of Conceptual Process Modelling.

3.1.3 The role of Enquiry Access Paths in Validating the Logical Data Model

The definition of Enquiry Access Paths serves two purposes:

- validating the Required System Logical Data Model;
- creating structures for enquiry processes.

It is important to ensure that the data needed for the enquiry results can be retrieved. It is not essential to get the required presentation of the output reflected in the enquiry structure – the function that invokes the enquiry can format the data into the required output if necessary. For example, a function can sort, suppress duplicates, count and calculate derived data. This does not need to be done within the Enquiry Access Path.

Testing against requirements is where the Required System Logical Data Model is really defined. The initial Logical Data Model is only the analyst's subjective view but it must be tested against the requirements for information support before it can be regarded as correct. The development of Enquiry Access Paths is a formalised way of checking the Logical Data Model and should be seen as an important activity in the development of the Logical Data Model.

During the development of Enquiry Access Paths, if the Logical Data Model cannot support a retrieval requirement it should be modified so that it can provide the required data in the correct form.

If there are parts of the Logical Data Model that are not used by any of the Enquiry Access Paths, their inclusion in the Logical Data Model should be questioned.

There are some possibilities for trade-off in extending the Logical Data Model and manipulating retrieval results. Two reasonable guidelines are:

- define attributes such that, as far as possible, sets of entities can be retrieved directly by attribute value, rather than by some computed selection. For example, if an enquiry requires the retrieval of a set of entity occurrences where a date is later than a scheduled date, it is easier to select all entities with a status of 'late' rather than comparing the dates of all occurrences to the scheduled date. This requires the inclusion of a status within the required entity that can be set to 'late';
- where there is a simple choice between adding further structure to the Logical Data Model and manipulating the output, then choose to manipulate the output. It is generally better to keep the Logical Data Model as simple as possible.

3.2 Conceptual Process Modelling Technique

Although the products of Conceptual Process Modelling share some of the same notations, they are developed in slightly different ways. The techniques will therefore be described separately as follows:

- Developing Enquiry Access Paths;
- Developing Effect Correspondence Diagrams;
- Developing Enquiry Process Models;
- Developing Update Process Models.

3.2.1 Developing Enquiry Access Paths

The development of Enquiry Access Paths consists of a number of activities as represented in Figure 3-5.

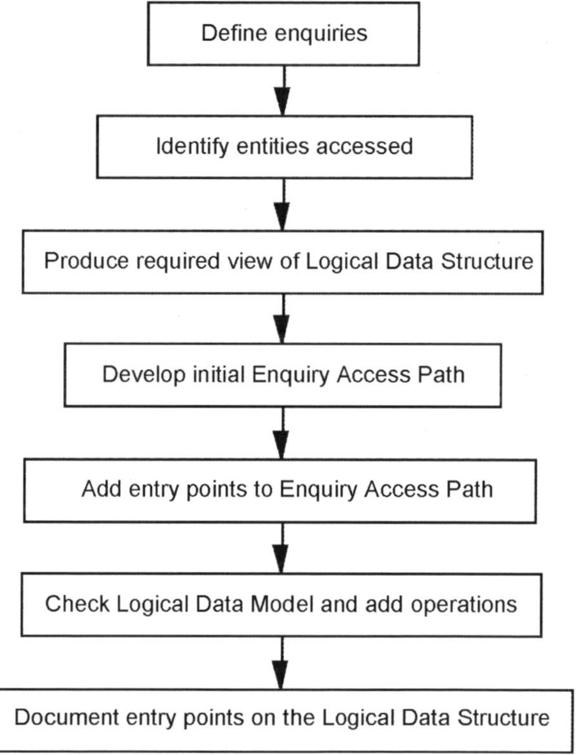

Figure 3-5 Activities in developing Enquiry Access Paths

These activities are described in the following paragraphs.

Define Enquiries

Enquiries are derived principally from the Requirements Catalogue (see Chapter 2). Enquiries are identified with reference to the information support needed by business activities. Common enquiries can be identified as re-usable components which are used within functions, event processes and other enquiries.

Enquiries are documented initially on the Entity Access Matrix and in the Event and Enquiry Catalogue. Each enquiry must be identifiable by a unique name.

For each enquiry, it is necessary to identify the data items that are required as output. Where I/O Structures have already been developed for the function to which the enquiry belongs, these can be used as a source of the data items for the enquiry.

Enquiry triggers are specified as the information that can be provided to the enquiry in order for the system to generate the required information for output to the user. For example, if a user of the EU-Rent system needs to find out whether it is possible to satisfy a rental request, he/she needs the system to list out all available cars by inputting the required car group at a specified branch.

The trigger includes the selection criteria for the entity which is nominated as the entry point for the enquiry. There may be more than one candidate entry point for a particular enquiry, one of which should be selected as the entry point to be used. For example, in the EU-Rent system, the simple enquiry to list out all available cars of a particular car group at a particular branch could have either Branch or Car Group as the entry point. Alternatively the trigger can be a non-unique attribute or set of primary keys which identify a set of occurrences.

The enquiry trigger may also contain selection criteria for other entities included in the enquiry.

The enquiry trigger is documented in the Event and Enquiry Catalogue. The enquiry trigger is usually also documented as a list of input items on the Enquiry Access Path. Note that enquiry triggers may contain parameters as well as items of data, for example, ranges of values for attributes.

Identify Entities Accessed

By looking at the Entity Access Matrix and the data required for output, it is possible to identify which entities are required to be accessed by this enquiry. At this point, if any of the data cannot be derived from the Logical Data Model, this must be resolved before proceeding further.

Produce Required View of Logical Data Structure

This activity may either be done by developing a separate diagram or by annotating the Logical Data Structure.

Starting from the entry point:

- show each access down a relationship (i.e., master to detail) vertically;
- show each access up a relationship (i.e., detail to master) horizontally.

A simple example of a required view of a Logical Data Structure is given in Figure 3-6 for the enquiry outlined above.

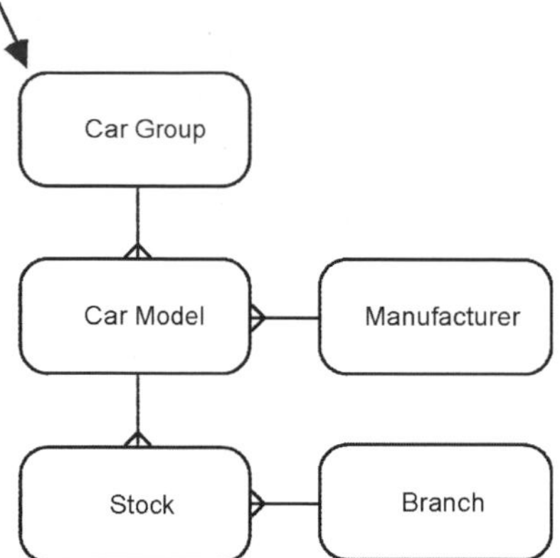

Figure 3-6 Required view of Logical Data Structure for enquiry on manufacturers for models within a specified car group

Develop Initial Enquiry Access Path

The required view of the Logical Data Structure can be converted into an initial Enquiry Access Path by doing the following:

- show downward accesses as iterations, i.e., as a 'set' of reads;
- add selections where necessary.

If more than one entity occurrence needs to be read, then an iterative structure is required. The entity name is placed in the iterated box and the box above contains 'Set of' with the entity name.

The initial Enquiry Access Path for the example required view of the Logical Data Structure shown in Figure 3-6 is shown in Figure 3-7.

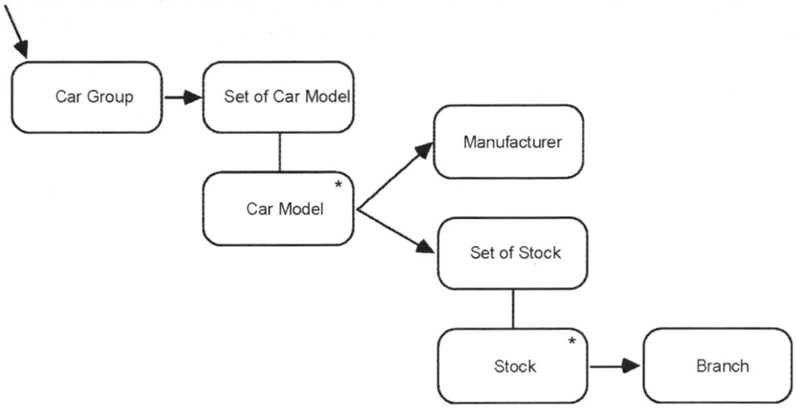

Figure 3-7 Example initial Enquiry Access Path

Add Entry Points to the Enquiry Access Path

List the key, or non-key, attributes used for entry next to the arrow to the entry point entity (these attributes must be part of the enquiry trigger).

There are two kinds of entry point:

- unique occurrence;
- multiple occurrence.

In the first case, the Enquiry Access Path is simply annotated with the name of the primary key or other candidate key as one of the items on the entry arrow.

In the second case, where multiple occurrences of the first entity are to be accessed, an iteration needs to be added above the entry point entity. For example, for an enquiry that requires a listing of all rentals with the same return date, the enquiry data will include the date and the entry point will be an iteration of rentals as shown in Figure 3-8.

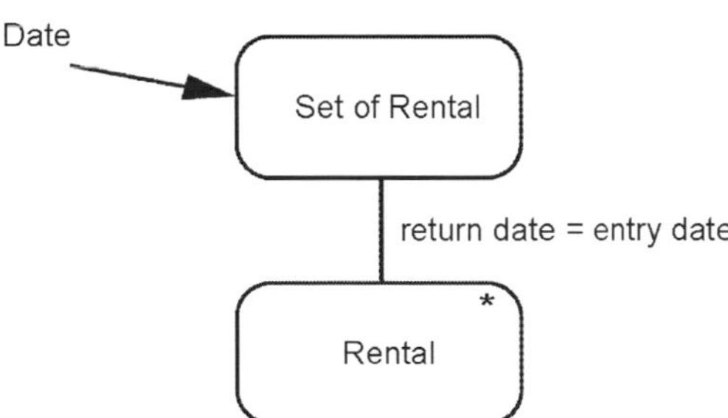

Figure 3-8 Iterated entry point

The example above shows an iterated entry point. The condition on the iteration ensures that each occurrence of Rental accessed will have a date the same as the date required. Conditions are explained later in this chapter.

Where all occurrences of the entry point entity are required, without any input parameters defining sub-sets required, the entry arrow can be left blank.

Check Logical Data Model and add operations

After the entry points have been established, check that all the required data can be obtained using the following kinds of read operation:

- read entity directly using key;
- read next detail entity of a master entity;
- read master entity of detail entity.

If the Enquiry Access Path does not deliver the required data in the correct access grouping or level of detail required, the following actions can be taken:

- modify the Logical Data Model to ensure that the data content can be derived and adequate relationships exist for the required navigation paths;
- restructure the Enquiry Access Path.

If the data needs to be sorted or calculated, operations should be added to the Enquiry Access Path to perform these actions (see 'define' operation described above).

Operations should only be added if they are thought useful for the future development of the enquiry.

The example Enquiry Access Path shown above in Figure 3-7 is annotated with operations as shown in Figure 3-9.

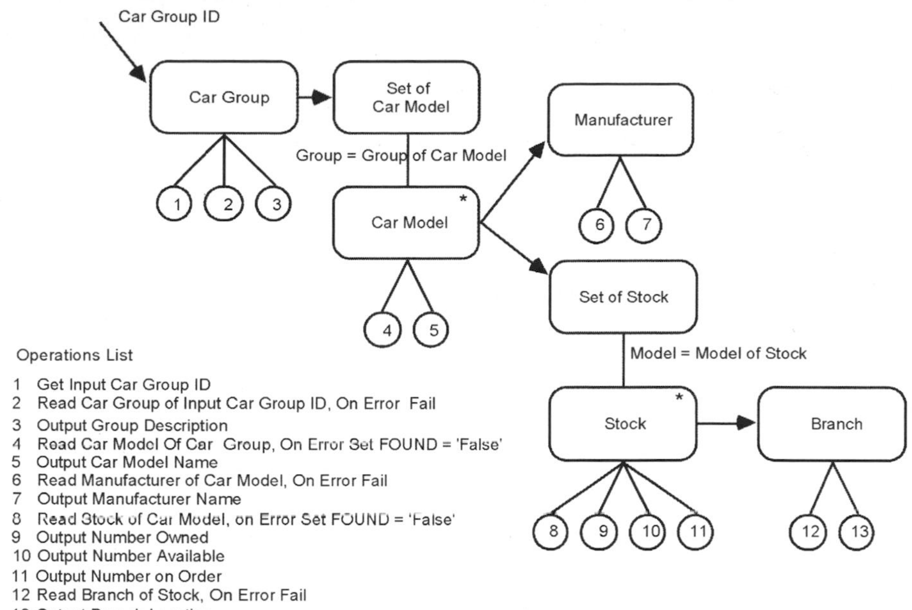
Car Group ID
Car Group
Set of Car Model
Group = Group of Car Model
Car Model
Manufacturer
Set of Stock
Model = Model of Stock
Stock
Branch
Operations List
1 Get Input Car Group ID
2 Read Car Group of Input Car Group ID, On Error Fail
3 Output Group Description
4 Read Car Model Of Car Group, On Error Set FOUND = 'False'
5 Output Car Model Name
6 Read Manufacturer of Car Model, On Error Fail
7 Output Manufacturer Name
8 Read Stock of Car Model, on Error Set FOUND = 'False'
9 Output Number Owned
10 Output Number Available
11 Output Number on Order
12 Read Branch of Stock, On Error Fail
13 Output Branch Location

Figure 3-9 Enquiry Access Path with operations

Document entry points on the Logical Data Model

In order that physical data design can be carried out, all the entry points to the Logical Data Model need to be identified. These can be shown diagrammatically as arrows pointing to the relevant entities, annotated with the relevant data items on the Required System Logical Data Structure diagram.

Other considerations in developing Enquiry Access Paths

Derived Data

In the example above, it is necessary to retrieve the number owned and number on order for all stock items. Suppose that 'Number Owned' and 'Number on Order' are not attributes of Stock, but need to be derived. The partial Logical Data Structure shown in Figure 3-10 illustrates how this might be done.

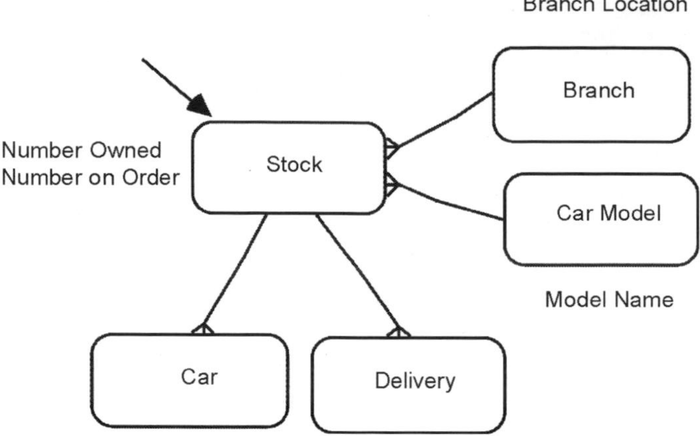

Figure 3-10 Required View Logical Data Structure showing entities needed to calculate Stock

In this Logical Data Structure, the Car and Delivery entities are required – the count of the occurrences of the Car entity will give the number owned and the number on order can be derived by looking at the Delivery entity. The Enquiry Access Path for this enquiry is shown in Figure 3-11.

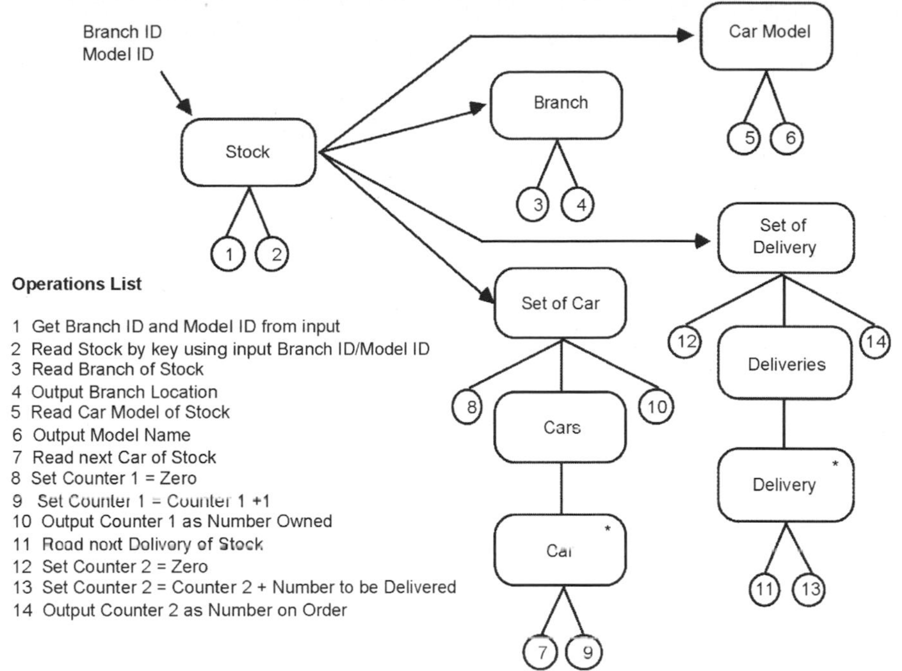

Branch ID
Model ID
Stock
Branch
Car Model
Set of Delivery
Set of Car
Cars
Car
Deliveries
Delivery
Operations List
1 Get Branch ID and Model ID from input
2 Read Stock by key using input Branch ID/Model ID
3 Read Branch of Stock
4 Output Branch Location
5 Read Car Model of Stock
6 Output Model Name
7 Read next Car of Stock
8 Set Counter 1 = Zero
9 Set Counter 1 = Counter 1 +1
10 Output Counter 1 as Number Owned
11 Read next Delivery of Stock
12 Set Counter 2 = Zero
13 Set Counter 2 = Counter 2 + Number to be Delivered
14 Output Counter 2 as Number on Order

Figure 3-11 Enquiry Access path showing derived data

Note that a convention has been used in this and subsequent diagrams which has not been previously described. An extra structure box has been inserted between the 'set of' box and the box representing the repeated access for both iterations. This extra box is inserted so that a clear sequence is shown with the operations under the 'set of' boxes. Adding an extra box in this way ensures that the Enquiry Access Path more closely resembles a Jackson-like structure which can more readily be converted directly into a program design.

Selection based on entity content (state or attribute value)

Suppose we wanted, as in the previous example, to derive Number Owned and Number Available for Stock. We would need to introduce a selection on Car as shown in Figure 3-12.

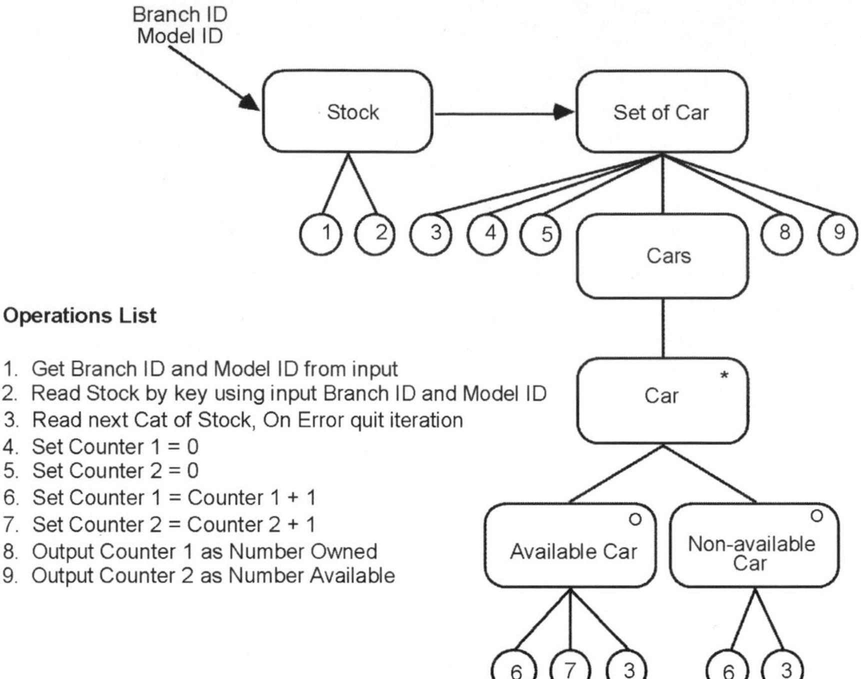

Branch ID
Model ID
Stock
Set of Car
1
2
3
4
5
Cars
8
9
Operations List
1. Get Branch ID and Model ID from input
2. Read Stock by key using input Branch ID and Model ID
3. Read next Cat of Stock, On Error quit iteration
4. Set Counter 1 = 0
5. Set Counter 2 = 0
6. Set Counter 1 = Counter 1 + 1
7. Set Counter 2 = Counter 2 + 1
8. Output Counter 1 as Number Owned
9. Output Counter 2 as Number Available
Car *
Available Car o
Non-available Car o
6
7
3
6
3

Figure 3-12 Selection added to Car

In this example, the operations are added to the iteration (the 'set of' box) so that the first occurrence of the Car entity is read before the iteration is initiated. If there are no Car entity occurrences, the counters are not incremented. This is known as the 'read-ahead/read-replace' convention for the iterated read.

An alternative way of representing the enquiry in Figure 3-12 is shown in Figure 3-13.

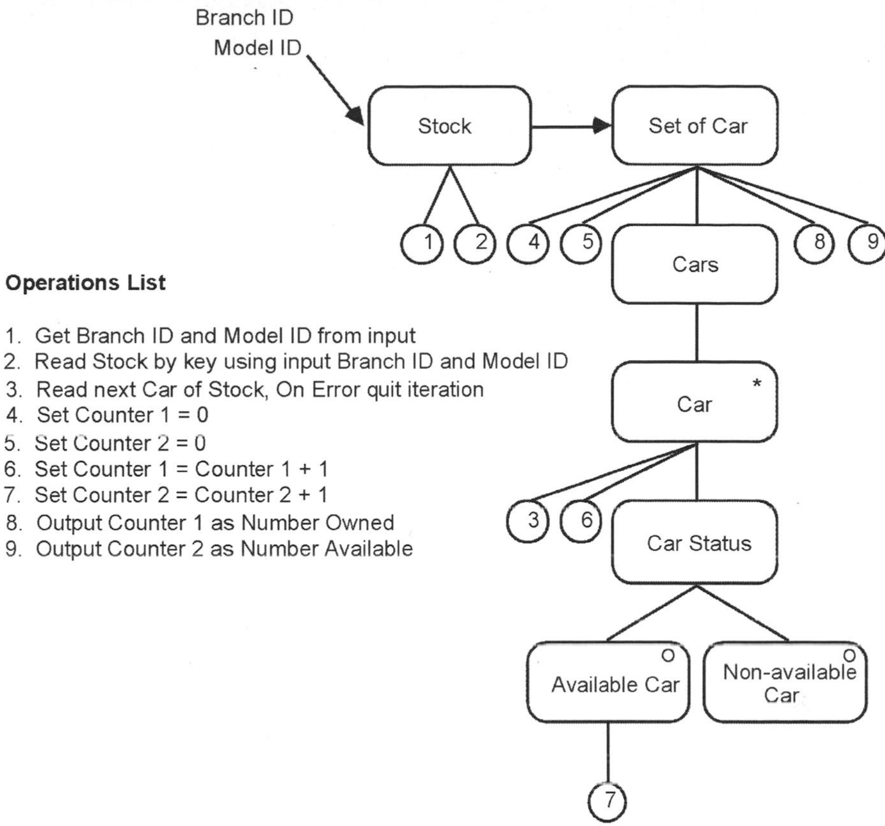
Branch ID
Model ID
Stock
Set of Car
1
2
4
5
Cars
8
9
Operations List
1. Get Branch ID and Model ID from input
2. Read Stock by key using input Branch ID and Model ID
3. Read next Car of Stock, On Error quit iteration
4. Set Counter 1 = 0
5. Set Counter 2 = 0
6. Set Counter 1 = Counter 1 + 1
7. Set Counter 2 = Counter 2 + 1
8. Output Counter 1 as Number Owned
9. Output Counter 2 as Number Available
Car *
3
6
Car Status
Available Car O
Non-available Car O
7

Figure 3-13 Alternative to Figure 3-12

Note that the convention of adding an extra box has been extended to include a selection as well as an iteration in this example.

Adding Conditions

It is useful to add conditions on selections and iterations to specify under what circumstances an iteration will take place and to specify the circumstances under which one option of a selection will be chosen rather than the others.

A condition is added to the iteration and selection in Figure 3-12 as shown in Figure 3-14.

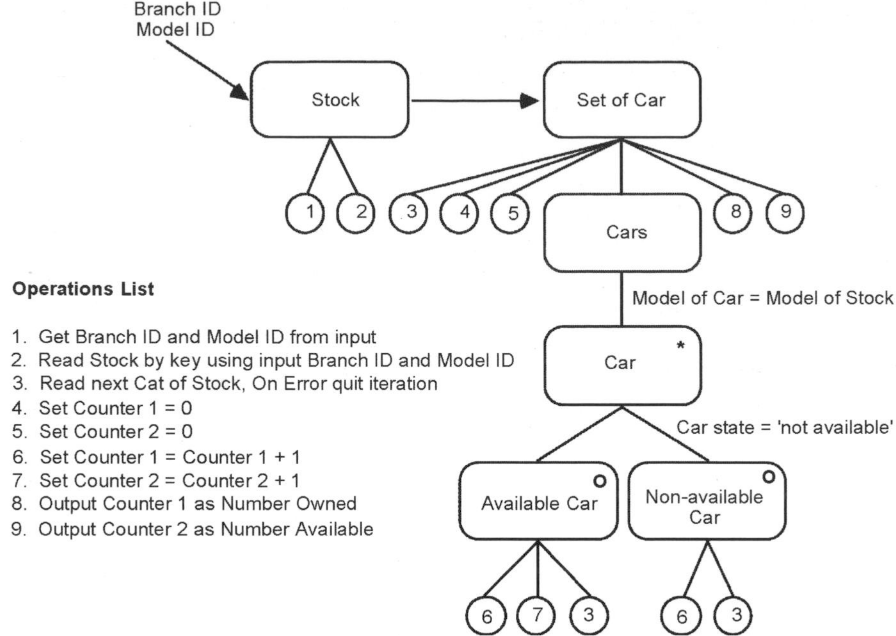
Branch ID
Model ID
Stock
Set of Car
1
2
3
4
5
Cars
8
9
Operations List
1. Get Branch ID and Model ID from input
2. Read Stock by key using input Branch ID and Model ID
3. Read next Cat of Stock, On Error quit iteration
4. Set Counter 1 = 0
5. Set Counter 2 = 0
6. Set Counter 1 = Counter 1 + 1
7. Set Counter 2 = Counter 2 + 1
8. Output Counter 1 as Number Owned
9. Output Counter 2 as Number Available
Model of Car = Model of Stock
Car *
Car state = 'not available'
Available Car o
Non-available Car o
6
7
3
6
3

Figure 3-14 Addition of conditions to iteration and selection on Enquiry Access Path

This example makes it clear under what circumstances the iterated part is repeated and links the condition to the operation which reads occurrences of the Car entity. Walking through the Enquiry Access Path, the various occurrences of the Car entity are read and with each successive read the condition is tested to see if there is a failure in the read operation. With each repetition of the operation, the condition is tested. If the condition fails, the iteration is terminated.

Exclusive Relationships

Where an access path encounters an exclusive relationship, a selection is added to the Enquiry Access Path to denote that either one or the other will be accessed. An example of an exclusive relationship in the EU-Rent Logical Data Model is shown in Figure 3-15.

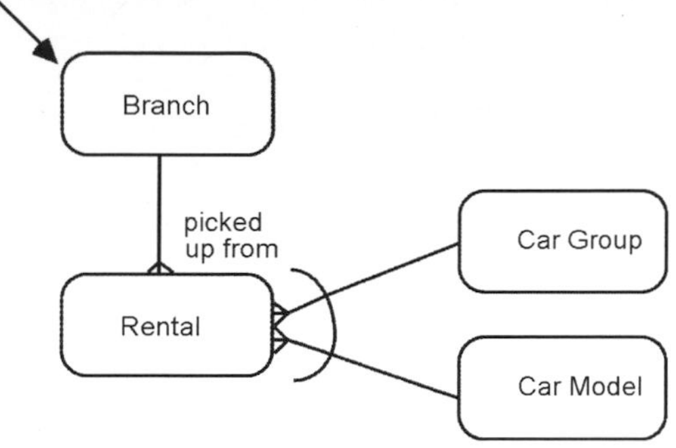

Figure 3-15 Partial Logical Data Structure with Exclusive Relationship

This Required View is converted into the Enquiry Access Path shown in Figure 3-16.

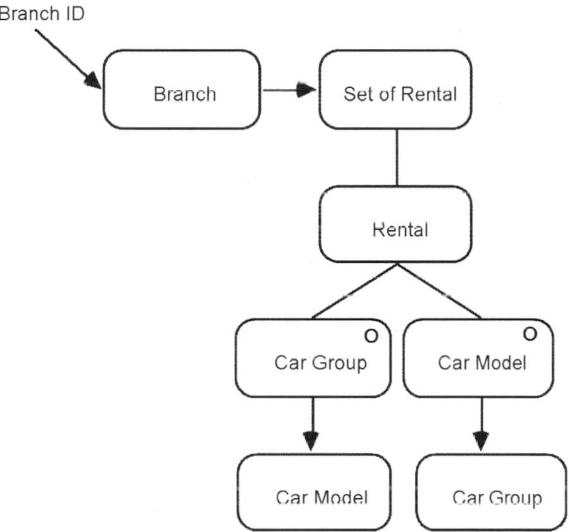

Figure 3-16 Enquiry Access Path with selection representing exclusive relationships

3.2.2 Developing Effect Correspondence Diagrams

The Effect Correspondence Diagramming technique is used to provide the detailed system processing by defining the effects on entities for each event.

This activity is an important technique for validating the results of Entity Life History Analysis. As a consequence Effect Correspondence Diagrams are often developed in parallel with Entity Life Histories.

An Effect Correspondence Diagram is drawn for each event. Each effect of the event shown on Entity Life Histories should be included with accesses for navigation and reads. Event data comprising attributes input to the update process need to be specified. Normally this will be the entity key which is the entry point to the Logical Data Model, plus some updating information.

Effect Correspondence Diagrams can be developed following the steps shown in Figure 3-17.

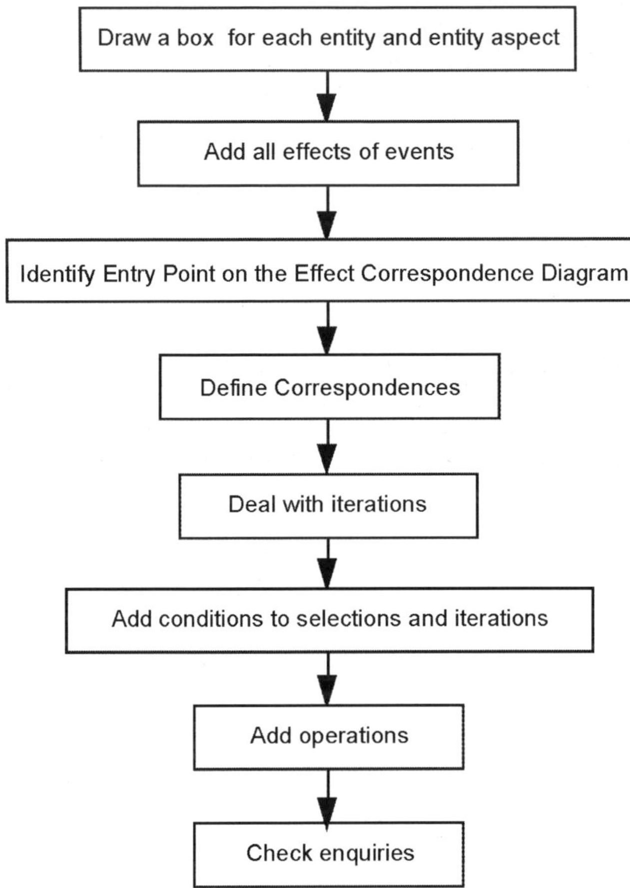

Figure 3-17 Steps in development of Effect Correspondence Diagrams

These steps are described in more detail in the following paragraphs and illustrated using an example from the EU-Rent system. The partial Logical Data Structure for this example is shown in Figure 1-3.

The Entity Access Matrix for the event 'Car Write-off' shows the following entries:

Entity	Effect type
Car	Death, Cut
Car Booking – general	Death
Car Booking – special (assignment, transfer, service)	Death
Branch	Lose
Car Group	Lose
Rental	Lose

Before starting to build the Effect Correspondence Diagram, it is important to refer to the description of the event in the Event and Enquiry Catalogue to get an overview of what the event is achieving and to derive the input data. It is useful to build a mental picture of the progress of the event when building up an Effect Correspondence Diagram – this should not be a mechanical process, but is a useful technique for cross-checking the results of the analysis so far.

Draw a box for each entity and entity aspect

Draw a box for each entity and entity aspect with an entry in the Entity Access Matrix.

Each gain (G) and lose (L) entry should be investigated further before being added to the diagram. Where there is a Gain or Lose on the Entity Access Matrix, the Entity Life Histories for those entities should be examined to see if the gain or loss is included as an effect. If so, then the effect is included on the Effect Correspondence Diagram. If not, it should be excluded.

Entity sub and super-types should be treated in the following way. The effect on the super-type is shown as distinct from the effect(s) on the sub-types. At this stage, separate boxes should be drawn – one for the super-type and one representing the group of sub-types.

The initial diagram for the Car Write-off event is shown in Figure 1-3.

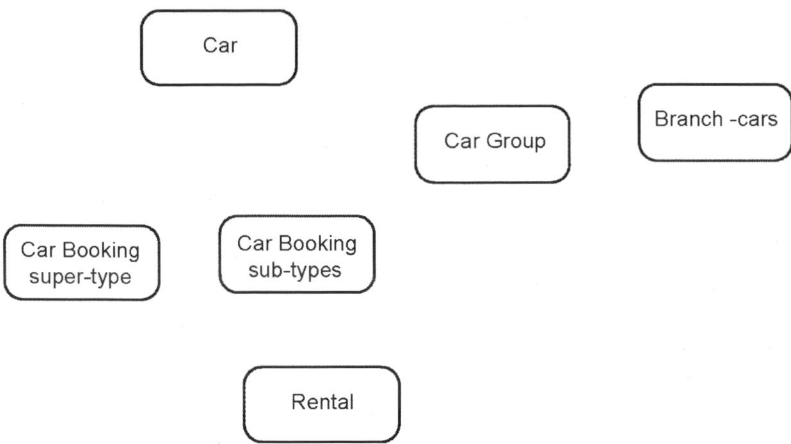

Figure 3-18 Initial Diagram for Car Write-off Effect Correspondence Diagram

This example shows the Car Booking super-type as one box and a single box is shown representing all the sub-types of Car Booking.

Add all effects of events

All the different effects of this event on these entities should now be added to the diagram. These can be derived by looking through the Entity Life Histories of these entities and finding out how many times the event appears on the diagram. Alternatively, some CASE tools may be able to report this information directly based upon the Entity Life History information.

If there are multiple effects of the event on an entity:

- if they are alternative effects (indicated by effect qualifiers), create a selection on the Effect Correspondence Diagram under the entity box already there;
- if they are simultaneous effects (indicated by entity roles), create a separate box for each entity role. If it is thought to be useful, a larger box can be drawn on the diagram enclosing simultaneous effects – this is not a mandatory notation.

If effect qualifiers and role names have been included on the Entity Life Histories, this should be a relatively straightforward process. A CASE tool may be able to provide the analyst with some assistance in doing this.

The Effect Correspondence Diagram for Car Write-off is amended as shown in Figure 3-19.

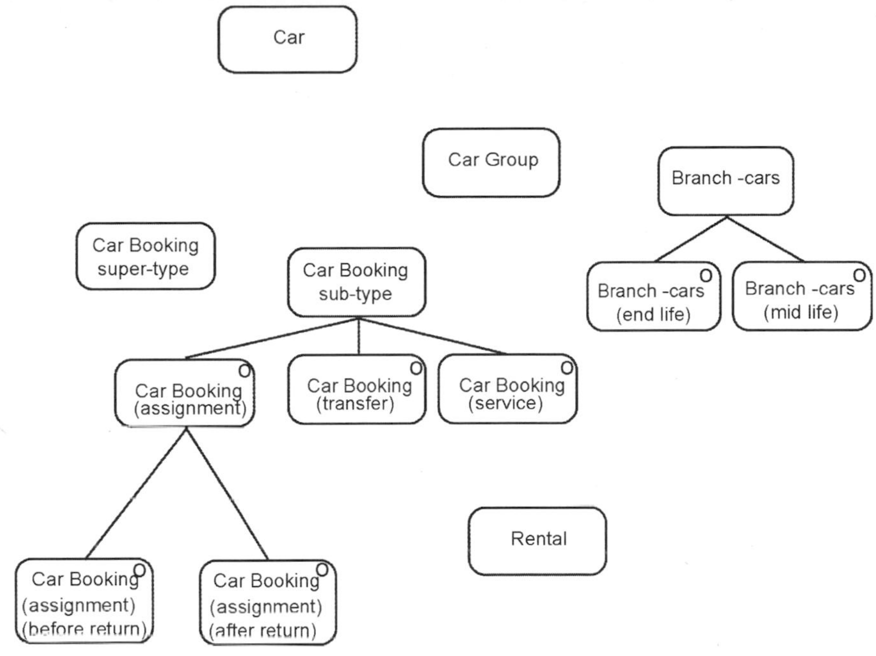

Figure 3-19 Effects added in to Effect Correspondence Diagram

Note that the effects on the three sub-types of Car Booking have been included as options below the box representing the sub-types.

Identify entry point on the Effect Correspondence Diagram

The entry point is defined as the first entity to be selected, using the input data. In the example above, the entry point is Car.

Define correspondences

Working from the entry point, define correspondences between effects. This should be done by 'walking through' the way in which the event will navigate the Logical Data Model. This is very likely to identify any missing effects or accesses required to entities for navigation. These should be added in at this point, ensuring the Entity Access Matrix is updated.

Correspondences are identified as one-to-one relationships between effects. Each correspondence should ideally relate to a relationship on the Logical Data Structure. The exception to this is where direct navigation is possible because the primary key of more than one entity has been supplied with the event data or the key of one entity can be used to directly select another entity (further up the hierarchy on the Logical Data Structure); for example, it is possible to directly select a Car Group from a given Car, even though they are not directly connected on the Logical Data Model.

Correspondences are marked with a one-directional arrow, showing the direction of navigation through the Logical Data Structure from the entry point.

The Effect Correspondence Diagram for Car Write-off is updated as shown in Figure 3-20.

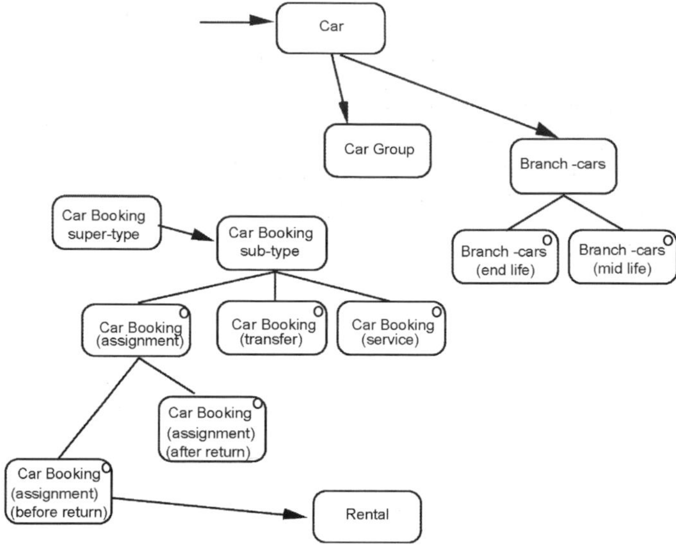

Figure 3-20 Correspondences marked between effects

Deal with iterations

Where a one-to-many relationship between a master and detail exists, and navigation is required from master to detail, the correspondence between then should be examined more closely:

- if only a single detail of the master is to be accessed, a one-to-one correspondence arrow should be placed between them. This occurs either where the key of the detail is provided as part of the event data or where some sort of condition will allow a single detail to be selected, for example, 'most recent occurrence';
- if more than one detail is to be accessed, a 'set of' box is placed as an iteration above the detail's effect. A correspondence can then be placed between the master's effect and the 'set of' box.

The updated Car Write-off Effect Correspondence Diagram is shown in Figure 3-21.

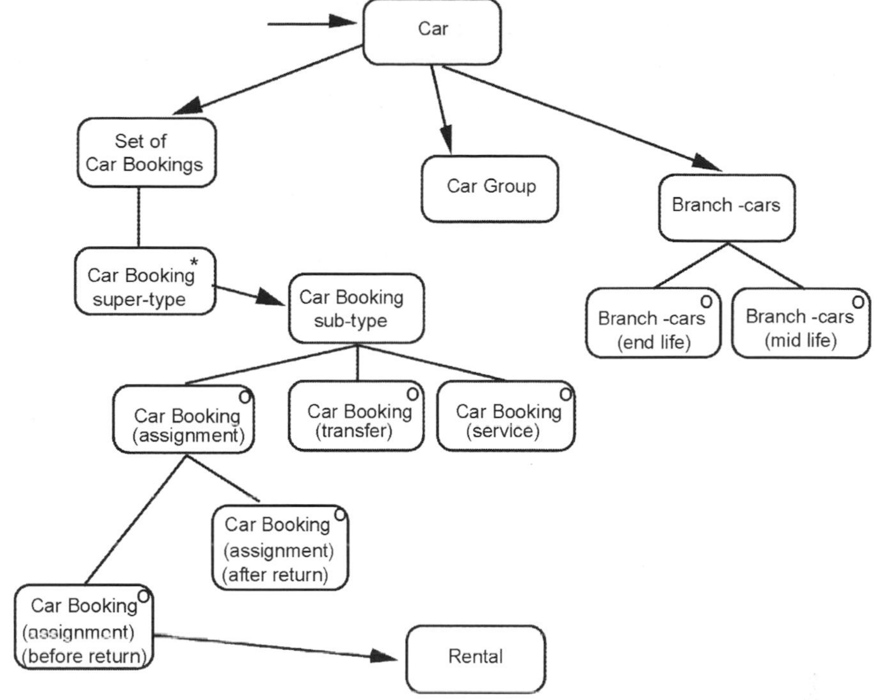

Figure 3-21 Effect Correspondence Diagram with 'set of' box

At this point, all correspondences should be one-to-one and the diagram should be supported by a workable navigation path through the Logical Data Structure, starting from the entry point.

Add conditions to selections and iterations

Conditions can be added to each option of a selection and each iteration. The condition should state the circumstances under which the option will be chosen or the iteration will be executed.

It is not necessary to add conditions to iterations where a complete set of detail entity occurrences are to be accessed. Similarly, it is not necessary to add conditions to the options that represent sub-types.

The Effect Correspondence Diagram for Car Write-off with conditions added is shown in Figure 3-21.

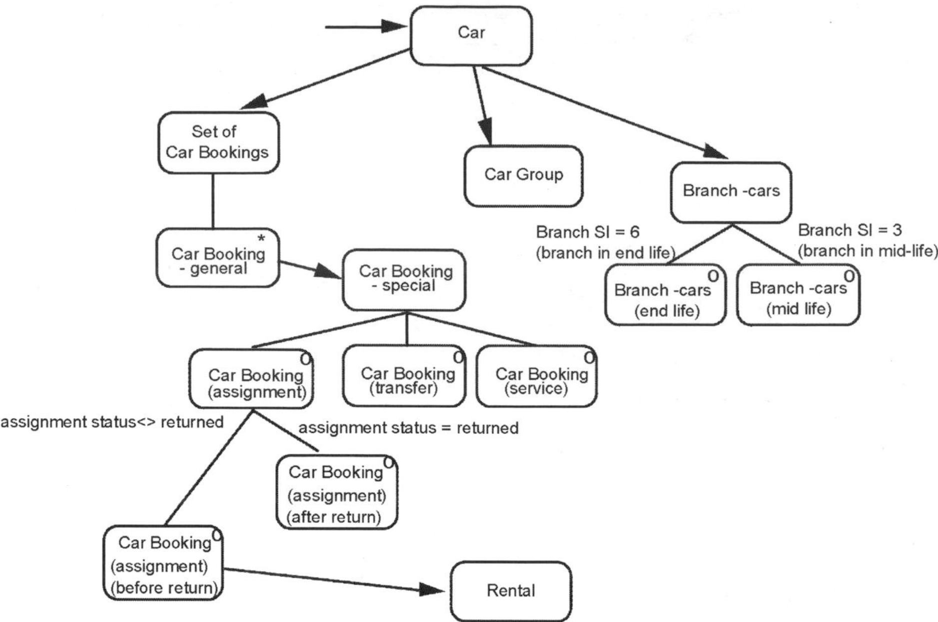

Figure 3-22 Car Write-off Effect Correspondence Diagram with conditions

Add operations

All effects that have been taken from Entity Life Histories will have a number of operations already associated with them, as shown on the Entity Life Histories. If thought useful for the future development of the event the operations should be copied directly across to the Effect Correspondence Diagrams for the appropriate effects. (Some CASE tools may be able to do this automatically.) It should be stressed that the effect that appears on an Entity Life History is the same as the effect when it appears on the Effect Correspondence Diagram. The only difference will be that the effect is identified by the event name on the Entity Life History and by the entity name on the Effect Correspondence Diagram.

Operations that were excluded from the Entity Life History are added to the Effect Correspondence Diagram at this point as follows:

- operations to read the entities;
- operation(s) to raise error(s) on an invalid state indicator (SI) value. These are created by examining the effect on the Entity Life History and considering the 'valid previous' SI values;
- operations which set the value of the entities' state indicators (SI). This is created by examining the effect on the ELH and using the 'set to' SI value;
- operations to write the entities.

Operations should be added to effects in the order in which they are to be executed. Operations can be added to nodes as well as effects on the diagram.

The Effect Correspondence Diagram for Car Write-off becomes rather complicated at this point, so the example of operations on an Effect Correspondence Diagram given in Figure 3-23 is for a simple event Rental Booking which assigns a specific car to a rental.

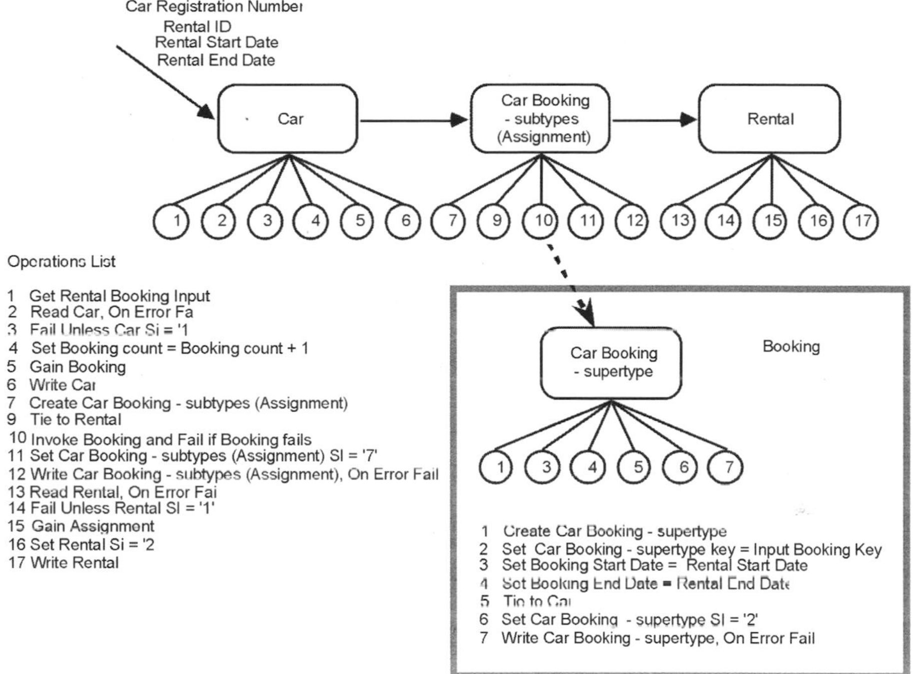

Figure 3-23 Example of Effect Correspondence Diagram with Operations

It is necessary to check the Effect Correspondence Diagram against the data content of the entities accessed to ensure that all operations can be supported.

For each effect on the Effect Correspondence Diagram:

- ensure that all the data needed for operations (including operations that output items for the event response data) are available, either in the entity, in the input data, or in entities somewhere along the correspondences between the entry point and this entity;
- if any operation cannot be supported, then:
  - if reference data is needed from another entity, add an operation invoking an enquiry process to obtain it; if this enquiry does not exist, add it to the Entity Access Matrix;
  - if derived data is needed, add operations to derive it. This may involve counts or summaries of sets (or selected subsets) of entity occurrences.

The data items required as input and generated as output should be documented for each effect/access on the Effect Correspondence Diagram. These items can be documented in the Effect Descriptions.

Check Enquiries

After all Effect Correspondence Diagrams have been completed, check the enquiries that were added to the Enquiry Access Matrix as a result of validating operations. If any are used only in one Effect Correspondence Diagram, add read-only effects to that diagram. If they are required from more than one Effect Correspondence Diagram, a reusable Enquiry Access Path should be specified which is invoked by an operation from the relevant effect.

Other considerations for Effect Correspondence Diagrams

Entity super and sub-types and Entity Aspects on Effect Correspondence Diagrams

Entity aspects always have a one-to-one relationship with one another. Therefore, if an event affects more than one aspect of the same entity, the effects will be in one-to-one correspondence.

Similarly, super-types always have a one-to-one relationship with its sub-types so where an event affects both super-type and sub-types, there will be a one-to-one correspondence between the super-type and a selection of the sub-types. However, the correspondence is often hidden in an invocation of a common process.

The Effect Correspondence Diagram for the event Rental Booking is shown in Figure 3-24. In this example, Rental Booking creates an Assignment, a sub-type of Car Booking. The effect on Assignment includes an invocation of the common process, Booking, which creates the super-type. The common process is also invoked by Transfer Booking and Service Booking (see Chapter 2).

Note that having distinct effects on the sub-type and super-type, each with a 'create' operation, does not imply any physical design decision as to whether sub-types and super-types will be implemented in the same table or different tables.

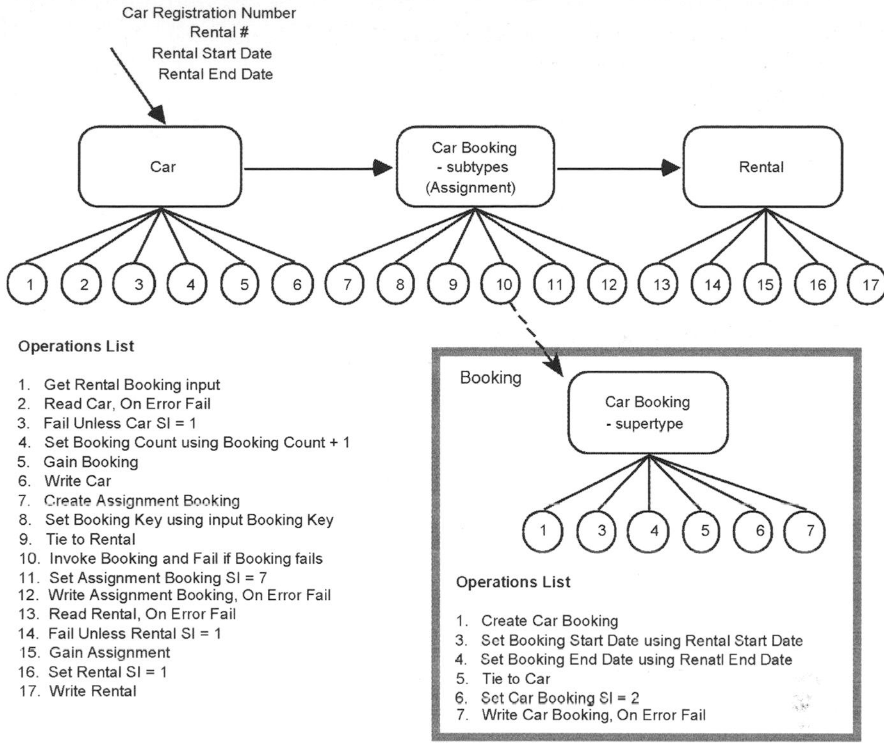

Figure 3-24 Effect Correspondence Diagram for Rental Booking

In practice the rental start and end dates are obtained by a pre-event enquiry which is also used in deciding which car to allocate. This enquiry is specified separately as a common Enquiry Access Path and will be referenced by this Effect Correspondence Diagram.

Informal alternative to using operations

Some projects may wish to customise their use of Effect Correspondence Diagrams and Enquiry Access Paths to provide a more informal specification. For example, if Enquiry Process Models and Update Process Models are to be produced, the Enquiry Access Paths and Effect Correspondence Diagrams may be left in a more simplified form. In this case, an alternative to the use of operations on Effect Correspondence Diagrams and Enquiry Access Paths would be to annotate effects and accesses with the access type (e.g. I (Insert), M (Modify), D (Delete), and R (Read)). There could also be local extensions to this where required.

Simultaneous Effects and Alternative Effects

Where an event affects an entity more than once in its life, the different effects are either denoted by effect qualifiers (as alternative effects) or by entity roles (as simultaneous effects).

Alternative effects are placed as options below the entity name in a box on the diagram. Simultaneous effects are separated out as different effects. If preferred, simultaneous effects can be enclosed in a larger box to denote the fact that they are treated together.

An example of alternative and simultaneous effects is given in Figure 3-25. In this example, two alternatives are given for the same Effect Correspondence Diagram, one of which uses the enclosing box to denote simultaneous effects and the other of which simply shows simultaneous effects as separate effects on the diagram. The event is Transfer Pick-up which causes ownership of a car to be transferred from one branch to another (Branch [old] and Branch [new]). The transfer from the old branch is either because the branch is at the end of its life or is during the middle of the branches life (Branch (end life) and Branch (mid life)).

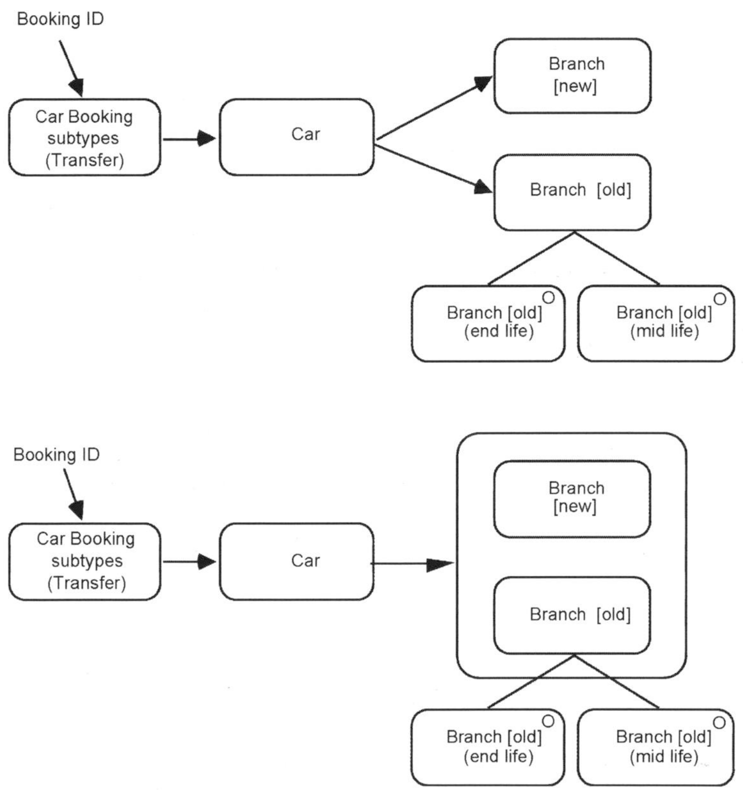

Figure 3-25 Examples of alternative and simultaneous effects including alternative representations for simultaneous effects

3.2.3 Developing Enquiry Process Models

Each Enquiry Access Path may be transformed, if required, into an Enquiry Process Model.

This is done using the following steps:

Group accesses on the Enquiry Access Path

The accesses in one-to-one correspondence on the Enquiry Access Path diagram are grouped. This is demonstrated for the enquiry Stocks and Manufacturers in Figure 3-26.

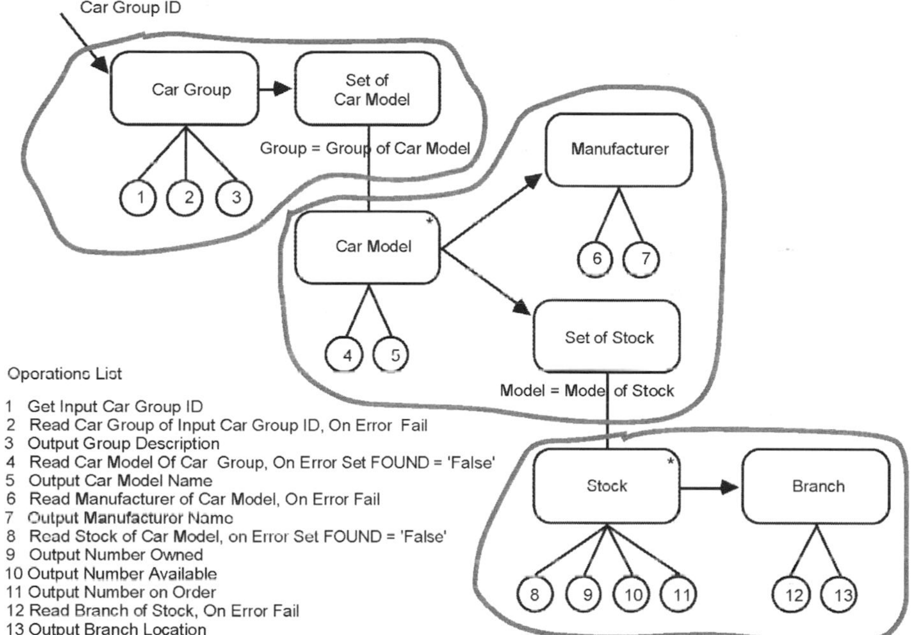
Car Group ID
Car Group
Set of Car Model
Group = Group of Car Model
Manufacturer
Car Model
Set of Stock
Model = Model of Stock
Stock
Branch
Operations List
1 Get Input Car Group ID
2 Read Car Group of Input Car Group ID, On Error Fail
3 Output Group Description
4 Read Car Model Of Car Group, On Error Set FOUND = 'False'
5 Output Car Model Name
6 Read Manufacturer of Car Model, On Error Fail
7 Output Manufacturer Name
8 Read Stock of Car Model, on Error Set FOUND = 'False'
9 Output Number Owned
10 Output Number Available
11 Output Number on Order
12 Read Branch of Stock, On Error Fail
13 Output Branch Location

Figure 3-26 Enquiry Access Path with grouped accesses

Convert to Jackson-like notation

The Enquiry Access Path diagram with grouped accesses is now converted into Jackson-like notation and all elementary and grouped accesses are represented as nodes on the Jackson structure diagram. Extra nodes may have to be inserted to adhere to strict Jackson structuring principles.

List the operations and allocate them to the structure

Operations from the Enquiry Access Paths are copied across (or re-presented if a CASE tool is used to achieve the transformation).

Allocate conditions to the structure

Conditions are allocated above each option of a selection, and above each iterated component. Conditions are taken across from the Enquiry Access Paths.

Walk through the structure

Walk through the structure, in order to check that the resultant sequence of processing makes sense. The Enquiry Process model developed from the example shown in Figure 3-26 is shown in Figure 3-27.

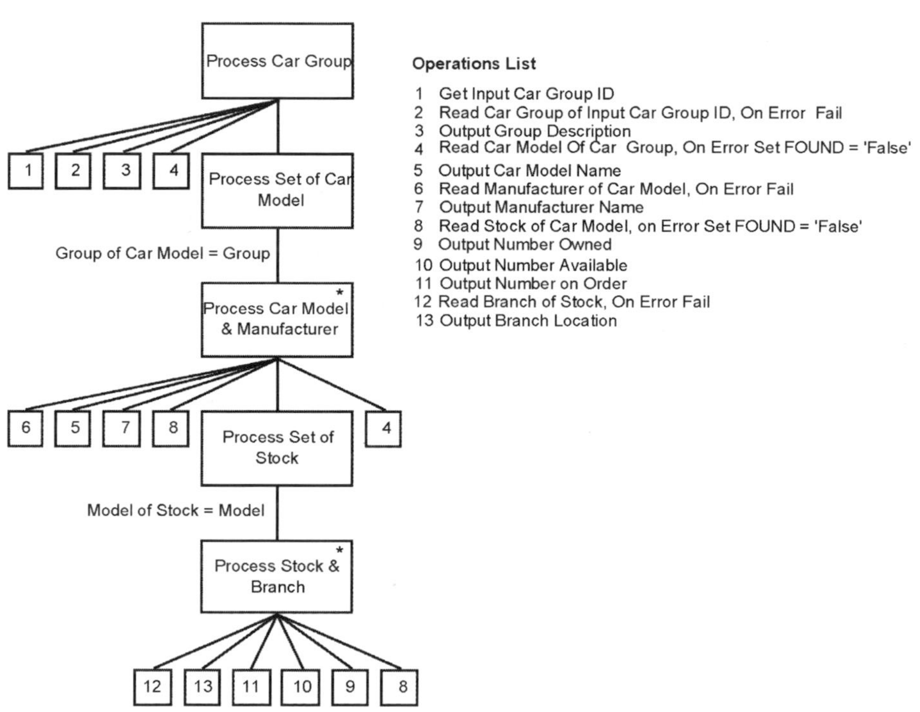
Process Car Group
1
2
3
4
Process Set of Car Model
Group of Car Model = Group
Process Car Model & Manufacturer *
6
5
7
8
Process Set of Stock
4
Model of Stock = Model
Process Stock & Branch *
12
13
11
10
9
8
Operations List
1 Get Input Car Group ID
2 Read Car Group of Input Car Group ID, On Error Fail
3 Output Group Description
4 Read Car Model Of Car Group, On Error Set FOUND = 'False'
5 Output Car Model Name
6 Read Manufacturer of Car Model, On Error Fail
7 Output Manufacturer Name
8 Read Stock of Car Model, on Error Set FOUND = 'False'
9 Output Number Owned
10 Output Number Available
11 Output Number on Order
12 Read Branch of Stock, On Error Fail
13 Output Branch Location

Figure 3-27 Example Enquiry Process Model for enquiry Stocks and Manufacturers

3.2.4 Developing Update Process Models

For each event which has been identified during Entity Life History analysis, a procedure to specify the update process is followed.

Group effects in one-to-one correspondence

Group the effects in one-to-one correspondence on the Effect Correspondence Diagram by drawing an enclosing box around all those effects. This is demonstrated in Figure 3-28 for the event Transfer Pick-up.

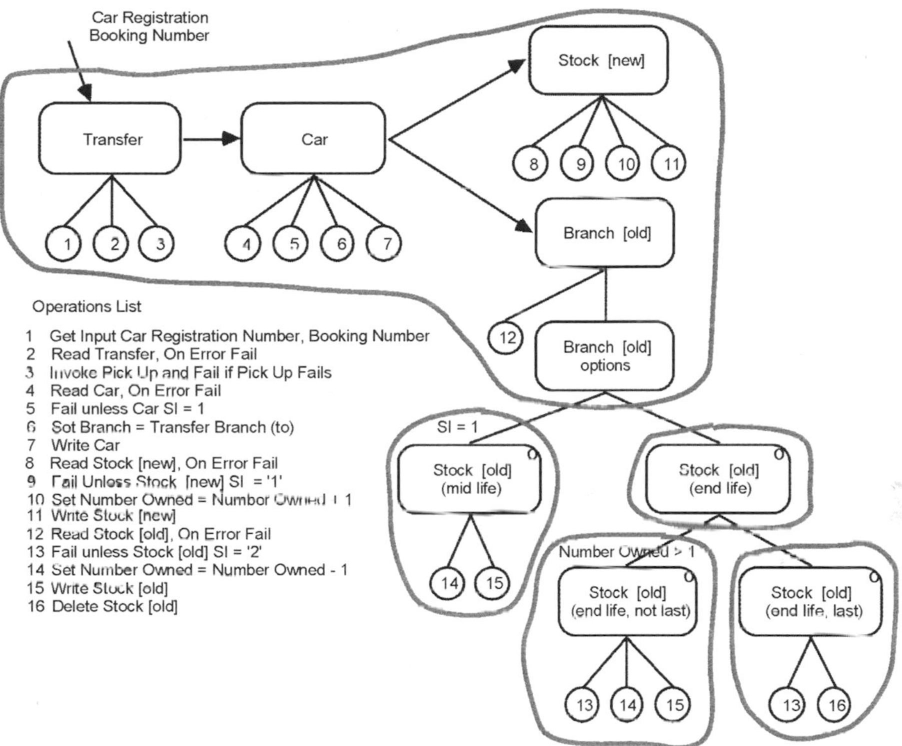
Car Registration
Booking Number
Transfer
Car
Stock [new]
8 9 10 11
Branch [old]
1 2 3
4 5 6 7
12
Branch [old] options
SI = 1
Stock [old] (mid life)
Stock [old] (end life)
14 15
Number Owned > 1
Stock [old] (end life, not last)
Stock [old] (end life, last)
13 14 15
13 16
Operations List
1 Get Input Car Registration Number, Booking Number
2 Read Transfer, On Error Fail
3 Invoke Pick Up and Fail if Pick Up Fails
4 Read Car, On Error Fail
5 Fail unless Car SI = 1
6 Set Branch = Transfer Branch (to)
7 Write Car
8 Read Stock [new], On Error Fail
9 Fail Unless Stock [new] SI = '1'
10 Set Number Owned = Number Owned + 1
11 Write Stock [new]
12 Read Stock [old], On Error Fail
13 Fail unless Stock [old] SI = '2'
14 Set Number Owned = Number Owned - 1
15 Write Stock [old]
16 Delete Stock [old]

Figure 3-28 Example ECD with grouped correspondences

Name the grouped effects, and residual elementary effects, as processes. The name should reflect the overall processing which is carried out for the effect(s).

Convert to Jackson-like notation

The Effect Correspondence Diagram with grouped effects is now converted into Jackson-like notation.

Allocate operations to structure

The operations should be allocated to relevant nodes on the structure diagram, that is, those process nodes which represent the effect to which the operations apply. Operations for each entity should be allocated in the following sequence:

1 operations to read the entity;

2 operation(s) to raise error on invalid SI value after the read;

3 create operations;

4 (enhanced) operations from effects on the ELH for that entity;

5 an operation which sets the SI of the entity;

6 a write/delete operation for the entity.

Allocate conditions to structure

Conditions are allocated above each option of a selection, and above each iterated component as defined in the Effect Correspondence Diagram. Selection conditions often test the value of an entity's state indicator. Iteration conditions often test for 'end-of-data-set'.

Walk through the structure

Walk through the structure to check that the resultant processing sequence makes sense. The Update Process Model for the Effect Correspondence Diagram shown in Figure 3-28 is shown below.

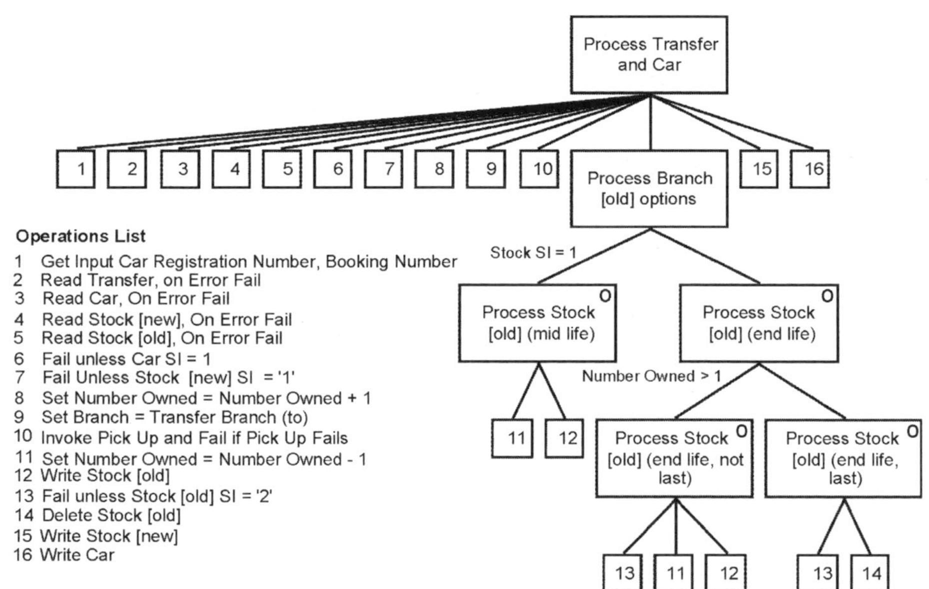
Process Transfer and Car
1
2
3
4
5
6
7
8
9
10
Process Branch [old] options
15
16
Operations List
1 Get Input Car Registration Number, Booking Number
2 Read Transfer, on Error Fail
3 Read Car, On Error Fail
4 Read Stock [new], On Error Fail
5 Read Stock [old], On Error Fail
6 Fail unless Car SI = 1
7 Fail Unless Stock [new] SI = '1'
8 Set Number Owned = Number Owned + 1
9 Set Branch = Transfer Branch (to)
10 Invoke Pick Up and Fail if Pick Up Fails
11 Set Number Owned = Number Owned - 1
12 Write Stock [old]
13 Fail unless Stock [old] SI = '2'
14 Delete Stock [old]
15 Write Stock [new]
16 Write Car
Stock SI = 1
Process Stock [old] (mid life) O
Process Stock [old] (end life) O
Number Owned > 1
11
12
Process Stock [old] (end life, not last) O
Process Stock [old] (end life, last) O
13
11
12
13
14

Figure 3-29 Example Update Process Model for Transfer Pick-Up

3.3 Relationship with other techniques

3.3.1 Entity Behaviour Modelling (covered in Chapter 2)

Entity Behaviour Modelling identifies events and enquiries and considers their interaction with entities. The interaction between events and entities is modelled using Entity Life Histories. Conceptual Process Modelling takes the products of Entity Behaviour Modelling and uses them directly to produce Enquiry Access Paths and Effect Correspondence Diagrams.

3.3.2 Function Definition (covered in the User Centred Design *and* Function Modelling *volumes)*

An event may be input via more than one function and so be listed on several Function Descriptions. For each function the analyst must check to see that the attributes for the event are contained in the input to or can be generated by the function.

After consultation with the user, output from Entity Behaviour Modelling will be used to update the Function Definition products by:

- adding newly identified events and enquiries to existing functions;
- identifying the need for new functions and input/output data.

Consistency checks are required to ensure that all events are assigned to the appropriate functions. In most cases assignment will be on a one-to-one basis but where more complex relationships exist between events and functions a function/event/enquiry matrix could be used to help in providing consistency.

Data items input to and output from functions should be checked against event and enquiry data to ensure consistency between them.

3.3.3 Logical Data Modelling (covered in the Data Modelling *volume)*

The Logical Data Structure is used to determine the correspondences between effects in Effect Correspondence Diagrams and Enquiry Access Paths. It is also used to check the data items used as event/enquiry data.

3.3.4 Physical Design (covered in the Database and Physical Process Design *volume)*

The Conceptual Process Modelling products are developed into physical specifications during Physical Process Specification.

Within a non-procedural (4GL style) environment it is often necessary to implement the logical database processes as 3GL components. However, if it is desired to generate physical database processes from non-procedural code, then the process models can be used as specifications, since they contain the essential information needed to specify a system in a non-procedural language.

In practice, it is often the Effect Correspondence Diagrams and Enquiry Access Paths that are used as the logical specification of the processing for input to physical design.

4 META-MODEL FOR BEHAVIOUR AND PROCESS MODELLING

The purpose of the concepts meta-model is to explain the concepts of Behaviour and Process Modelling in order to establish a common understanding between all parties interested in using and interpreting them. This model attempts to identify the key concepts and shows the interrelationships between the concepts..

The meta-model diagram is shown in Figure 4-1. Some points to note about the model are as follows:

- events and enquiries are defined as part of the same concept: Primary CM Process Trigger. The event or enquiry is seen as the trigger and the CM process is represented by the set of effects/accesses which result from this trigger;
- the concept of 'CM process trigger' has been sub-typed to show 'primary' and 'subsidiary' triggers. The primary trigger is recognised as an event or enquiry initiated externally or directly by the system. A subsidiary trigger is recognised by identifying substantial commonality between the effects of several primary process triggers. Where this commonality is generally recognised within the system, the common areas can be separately defined and named as CM process triggers in their own right. This type of CM process trigger can only be initiated by an effect of one of the primary process triggers from which it was identified, thus the mandatory one-to-one relationship between Subsidiary CM Process Trigger and Common Process Invocation;
- it is assumed that any number of effect correspondences can emanate from a specific effect/access but that only one correspondence can be 'to' an effect/access – this reflects the navigational aspect of Effect Correspondence Diagrams and Enquiry Access Paths;
- each operation is defined only once and then referenced by one or more effects/accesses – this encourages the perception that operations should be defined centrally and may appear on different design products - an operation is the same whether it appears on an Entity Life History, Effect Correspondence Diagram or Update Process Model. The majority of operations used can be specifically assigned to a single entity. Local identifiers can be added to entities to denote their context if required using the concept 'Operation Usage';
- 'state' as a concept is represented by a state indicator that is updated by effects of events/super-events. As can be seen by the model, a single state can be set by more than one effect indicating that effects under a zero-based iteration may leave the state unchanged and that effects under a selection may all set the state to the same value.

The model itself is followed by a table giving descriptions for each of the entities (concepts) on the diagram.

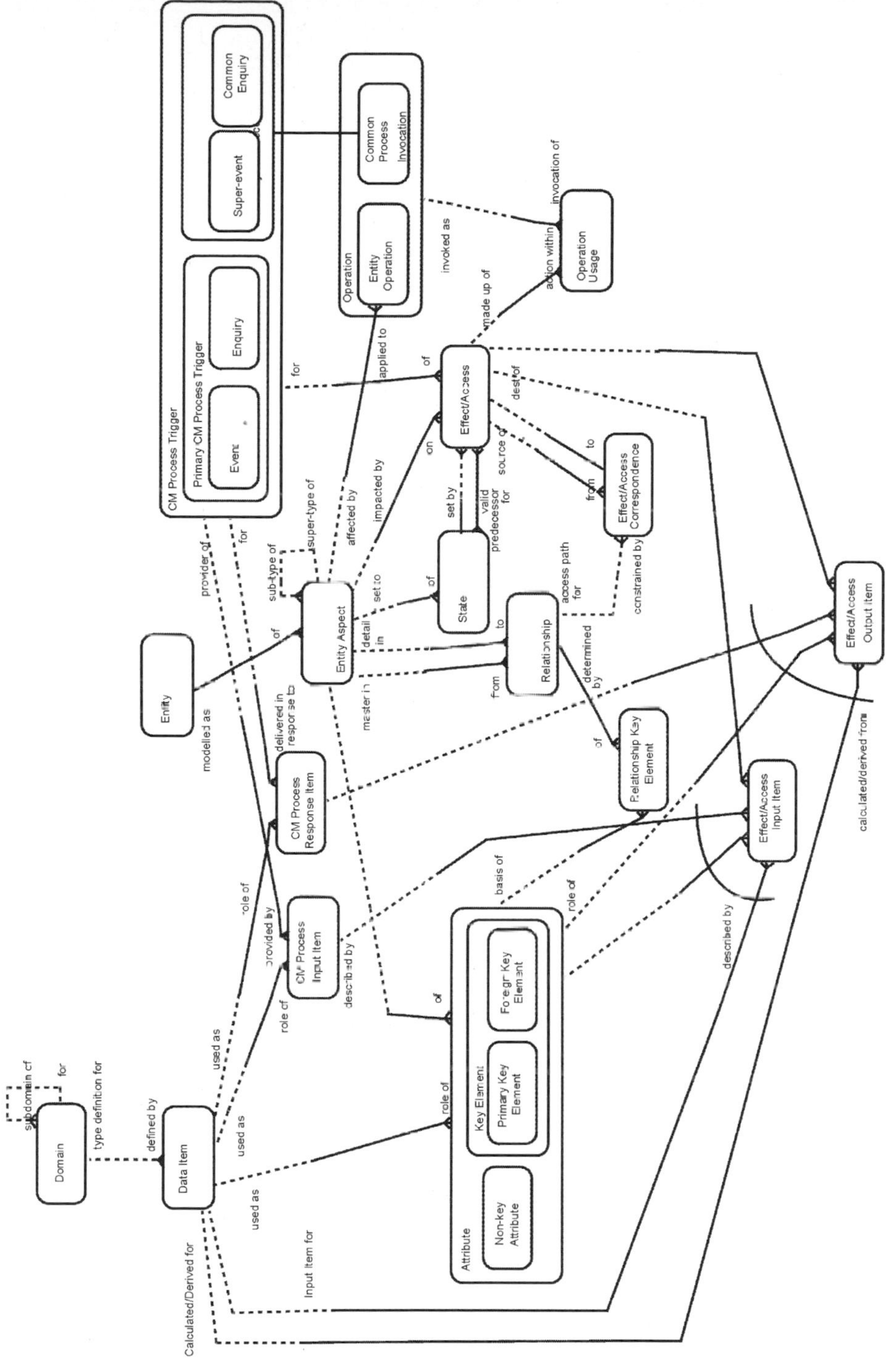

Figure 4-1 Meta-model of concepts covered by Modelling from the System's Perspective

Entity	Description
Attribute (super-type)	A characteristic property of an entity type, that is, any detail that serves to describe, qualify, identify, classify, quantify or express the state of an entity aspect. Each attribute is defined as belonging to only one entity aspect. Identifying attributes may appear in more than one entity description to support relationships. Each attribute is described by a data item which is the general definition of any element of data, wherever it is used.
CM Process Input Item	An element of data which is provided to a Conceptual Model Process by the CM Process Trigger (events and enquiries). Each element refers to a Data Item.
CM Process Response Item	An element of data which is output from a Conceptual Model Process in response to a CM Process Trigger (event or enquiry). Each element refers to a Data Item.
CM Process Trigger	The initiator of a process which accesses system data. This is a trigger within the Conceptual Model, not a business trigger. It is invoked by a function in the External Design or from within the Conceptual Model. Each primary trigger, together with the processing it invokes, is considered as a 'success unit' in that it cannot be subdivided into processes that are capable of being executed by themselves.
Common Enquiry	A common enquiry is an enquiry which is only ever invoked by other enquiries or events. It is defined separately as an enquiry and invoked by the other enquiries and/or events that use it. Each common enquiry should be identified and documented in the same way as all other enquiries. Common enquiries are modelling using Enquiry Access Paths.
Common Process Invocation	A type of operation which initiates a super-event or common enquiry within a process.
Data Item	Any element of data that is used within the system. Each data item may fulfil a number of different roles, each of which will be constrained by this central definition.
Domain	A set of characteristics shared by one or more Data Item.

Entity	Description
Effect/Access	The set of processing initiated by a Conceptual Model Process Trigger for a single entity aspect. Effects are the updating occurrences of this concept which are initiated by events.
Effect /Access Correspond-ence	A one-to-one relationship between effects/accesses. There are two types of correspondence represented by this concept: • single – between two single effects/accesses; • iterated between one single effect/access and a 'set of' another effect/access. An effect/access correspondence is directional and will almost always represent an access via a relationship on the Logical Data Model. The two relationships between this concept and 'Effect/Access' indicate that an effect/access may be the source of many correspondences but the destination of only one.
Effect /Access Input Item	A reference to a data item that is input to a specific effect/access. The item may have been input from a function (relationship to CM Process Input Item), from stored data (relationship to Attribute) or may have been derived as part of the event/access processing (relationship to Data Item).
Effect /Access Output Item	A reference to a data item that is output from a specific effect/access. The item may be output through a function (relationship to CM Process Input Item), to stored data (relationship to Attribute) or may be intermediate to be used as part of the event/access processing (relationship to Data Item).
Enquiry	A type of Primary CM Process Trigger which causes one or more entity aspects to be accessed but not updated.
Entity	Something, whether concrete or abstract, which is of relevance to the system and about which information needs to be stored. This concept represents a general definition of the entity that can be shared by a number of different systems/ areas. It is an aspect of the entity that is represented within a specific project's Logical Data Model.

Entity	Description
Entity Aspect	A view of an entity that is relevant to the system under investigation. There may be more than one aspect of the same entity represented on a single project's Logical Data Model. In most systems, only one aspect will need to be modelled so entity and aspect names are interchangeable.
Entity Operation	A type of operation which reads/changes attributes and/or relationships of a specific entity aspect.
Event	A type of Primary CM Process Trigger which causes changes to be made to attributes/relationships of one or more entity aspects.
Key Element	A type of attribute that is used as part of the primary key of one or more entity aspects or as a foreign key representing a relationship. These are the only types of attribute that can be included in more than one entity aspect.
Non-key attribute	A type of attribute which describes a characteristic of an entity but does not form part of the key structure. This type of attribute will belong to only one Entity Aspect.
Operation	An elementary piece of processing which is used in combination with other operations to make up effects/accesses. This concept represents the central definition of an operation which can be referenced by a number of different effects/accesses. Each operation will be defined once and referenced wherever it is used (for example, on an Entity Life History, an Effect Correspondence Diagram and Update Process Model).
Operation Usage	A cross-reference between effects/accesses and operations indicating that an operation can be included in more than one effect/access and an effect/access can cover a number of operations. This concept may hold a local identifier for the operation for the particular effect/access.
Primary CM Process Trigger	A type of CM Process Trigger which is initiated from the external design, time-triggered or system-triggered. The Effect Correspondence Diagram or Enquiry Access Path for this trigger will indicate data being supplied to the first node/effect/access from a source external to the process.

Entity	Description
Relationship	An association between two entity aspects (or an entity aspect and itself) to which all instances of the relationship must conform.
Relationship Key Element	The inclusion of a specific key element attribute in a specific relationship indicating the foreign key or cascading primary key structure within the Logical Data Model. (The key element attribute and the relationship connected using this concept must belong to the same entity aspect.)
State	A phase in the life of an entity aspect. The state of an entity aspect is altered in a predefined way each time the entity aspect is updated by effects of CM Process triggers. The value associated with each state is tracked using a State Indicator. Each updating effect will set the state indicator to a specific value. Any effect/access can 'test' the state indicator for a range of valid values before the processing of the effect/access can be initiated – updating effects must test the state to see if the update is permitted.
Subsidiary CM process Trigger	A type of CM process trigger which is recognised by identifying substantial commonality between the effects/accesses of several primary process triggers. Where this commonality is generally recognised within the system, the common areas can be separately defined and named as CM process triggers in their own right. This type of CM process trigger can only be initiated by an effect/access of one of the primary process triggers from which it was identified.
Super-event	If several different events have exactly the same effects on an entity at the same point in its life, the effects can be called by a name which describes them all – this is the super-event name.

5 PRODUCT DESCRIPTIONS FOR BEHAVIOUR AND PROCESS MODELLING

Listed below are the Product Descriptions for those products produced during Entity Behaviour Modelling and Conceptual Process Modelling. These Product Descriptions should not be regarded as definitive, rather they are a start point that can be tailored for each individual project. It is expected that each project will examine the composition list and add and remove as necessary to suit their particular project. In addition if a Case Tool is utilised then the Case Tool may have a suggested list of its own.

5.1 Effect Correspondence Diagrams (ECDs)

Purpose

To show the way in which effects for each event are related to one another and to demonstrate the navigation around the Required System Logical Data Model required to process the effects.

Suitability

The concept of an event as the unit of system processing is one of the underlying principles of computer system design, and Effect Correspondence diagrams support this view. Therefore Effect Correspondence Diagrams are suitable in all situations where predefined updates can be identified. They are suitable for specification of processes in 3GL, 4GL, distributed, object oriented and Client Server implementation environments.

Composition

Diagram drawn for the event showing effects, accesses for read/navigation, structure boxes and correspondences between them.

Operations and conditions added to the diagram if thought useful and the Effect Correspondence Diagram is to be used as the specification of processing.

Event data showing attributes input to the update processing.

Position in System Development Template

Specification – Conceptual Model.

Quality Criteria

For each:

1. Has the event name been completed correctly for this diagram?
2. Does the Effect Correspondence Diagram show all the correspondences between effects?
3. Have all of the entities which are affected by one event been documented on the Effect Correspondence Diagram for that event?
4. Does the Effect Correspondence Diagram accurately reflect requirements?
5. Are all notational conventions adhered to?
6. Where 'invoke' operations are used, is there a specification of the invoked process?

For the set:

7. Is the set of Effect Correspondence Diagrams complete?

External Dependencies

Relevant users to provide full information about their processing requirements.

5.2 Enquiry Access Paths (EAPs)

Purpose

To develop structures for enquiry processes based upon the required navigation around the Required System Logical Data Model.

To validate the Required System Logical Data Model by checking that all required data is present and correctly structured.

Each enquiry is described in a single diagram.

Suitability

Enquiry Access Paths are suitable where access requirements can be defined in advance, such as with user definable queries. They are useful where there are pre-defined access requirements and a need to design data access components. Enquiry Access Paths are also suitable for validating the Logical Data Model for completeness and consistency.

Composition

Diagram drawn for the enquiry showing accesses for read/navigation, structure boxes and correspondences between them.

Operations and conditions added to the diagram if thought useful and the Enquiry Access Path is to be used as the specification of processing.

Enquiry data showing attributes input to the enquiry processing.

Position in System Development Template

Specification – Conceptual Model.

Quality Criteria:

1 Is the enquiry correctly identified and named?

2 Is the navigation path supported by the relationships on the Logical Data Model?

3 Does the description of access rights in the entity and attribute/data item descriptions support the accesses defined in the access path?

4 Are notational and syntax conventions used conformant with standard conventions?

5 Where 'invoke' operations are used, is there a specification of the invoked process?

External Dependencies

None.

5.3 Enquiry Process Models

Purpose

To model the required processing for enquiries expressed in Enquiry Access Paths in Jackson-like diagrams to act as an input to Physical Process Specification.

Each model represents the logical process structure of an enquiry, including the operations.

Suitability

Enquiry Process Models are most suitable as an extension to Enquiry Access Paths for function components which are to be coded procedurally, or where performance issues are of primary importance. They are also suitable where the integrity of the entities accessed is significant.

Enquiry Process Models are suitable where the :

- complexity of enquiry processes is high;
- availability, clarity and stability of requirements is high;
- specificity of information and business processes is high;
- stability of business processes is high.

Composition

Enquiry Process Structure:

- a diagrammatic representation using the concepts of sequence selection and iteration. Conditions can be added to iterations and selections.

Operations List consisting of multiple operations entries as follows:

- operation number/reference;
- operation description.

Position in System Development Template

Specification – Conceptual Model.

Quality Criteria:

For each:

1 Is the enquiry name completed and valid?

2 Is the notation correctly used within the structure diagram?

3 Are all the operations used at least once?

4 Are all the aspects of the data structures incorporated into the Enquiry Process Structure, or are the clashes highlighted?

For the set:

5 Is this a complete set of documentation for all identified enquiry processes?

External Dependencies

None.

5.4 Entity Life Histories (ELHs)

Purpose

To chart the life of each entity in the Required System Logical Data Model from birth to death within a system in terms of the events which affect it. To model the constraints on updating of data required by the business which is to be supported by the new automated system. To identify events that have not been identified by examination of other SSADM products and to identify any changes required to the Logical Data Model to support the events.

Each entity is described by a single Entity Life History, and a set of these is packaged to provide this information for all entities.

Suitability

Events are key to successful system development in SSADM, from the identification of business events through to the success units in Physical Design. Entity Life Histories should be produced where the data updated by events is important. Entity Life Histories are critical where there are structured rules for data integrity and for large, complex update events. The product is also suitable where there is a need to look at the system from a time and exception perspective, enabling new business rules to be captured.

Entity Life Histories are suitable where the :

- complexity of data is high;
- complexity of functions is high.

Composition

For each entity, a diagram:

- with the entity name in the top box, below which a tree structure is drawn;
- which contains sequence, selection, iteration, parallel structures and quits and resumes;
- reflecting the effect(s) of each event on the entity (multiple effects are distinguished by effect qualifiers and/or entity roles);
- (if included) showing operations and state indicators for each effect;
- supported by a list of operations used on that diagram.

Position in System Development Template

Specification – Conceptual Model

Quality Criteria:

For each:

1. Does the entity name appear in the top box of the diagram?
2. Have all events which affect this entity (checked against the Entity Access Matrix) been documented on the Entity Life History?
3. Have multiple effects of a single event been distinguished by effect qualifiers and/or entity roles?
4. If being used, have all of the major operations been identified for each effect on the Entity Life History and correctly allocated?
5. Are all notational conventions adhered to?
6. Where Quit and Resume are used, is the quit from an assumed case to an alternative case?
7. Does the Entity Life History support the sequence of events required by the business?
8. Has the operations list been provided for this Entity Life History?
9. Have state indicators been included as appropriate?

External Dependencies

- Relevant users to provide full information about their processing requirements.
- Relevant users to join the Review Team.

5.5 Entity Access Matrix

Purpose

To ensure all events and enquiries affecting a Logical Data Model entity are captured. All Logical Data Structure entities must be accessed by one or more events or enquiries, otherwise they are not a necessary part of the required system.

Composition

Column headings: entity names.

Row headings: event or enquiry names.

Cell values as appropriate, indicating the type of effect or access.

Position in System Development Template

Specification – Conceptual Model

Quality Criteria:

1 Are all events and enquiries listed down the matrix side?

2 Are all Logical Data Model entities, entity aspects and sub-super-types listed across the matrix top?

3 Are all the cell entries either one of the appropriate actions or null?

4 Is there any event with no corresponding entity to act on?

5 Is there at least one create event for each entity?

External Dependencies

None.

5.6 Event and Enquiry Catalogue

Purpose

To describe important characteristics of all events and enquiries used in Entity Behaviour Modelling and Conceptual Process Modelling.

Composition

For each event/enquiry:

- Event/Enquiry ID;
- Event/Enquiry Name;
- Event/Enquiry Description;
- Business Activity/business event cross-reference;
- Average and Maximum occurrences;
- Data required as input to the event/enquiry;
- Entry point in to the Logical Data Model;
- Entities Accessed and access type.

Position in System Development Template

Specification – Conceptual Model

Quality Criteria:

1 Are all events and enquiries included in the catalogue?

2 Are all events and enquiries clearly described?

3 Is the catalogue consistent with the Entity Access Matrix?

External Dependencies

None.

5.7 Update Process Model

Purpose

To model the required processing for events expressed in Effect Correspondence Diagrams in Jackson-like diagrams to act as an input to Physical Process Specification. Each model represents the logical processing structure of an update process, including the operations. A processing model for an event is constructed by converting the Effect Correspondence Diagram for that event into a processing structure diagram.

Composition

Update Process Structure:

- a diagrammatic representation using the concepts of sequence selection and iteration. Conditions can be added to iterations and selections.

Operations List consisting of multiple operations entries as follows:

- operation number/reference;
- operation description.

Position in System Development Template

Specification – Conceptual Model

Quality Criteria:

For each:

1 Is the event name completed and correct?

2 Is the notation correctly used within the structure?

3 Are all the operations used at least once?

For the set:

5 Is this a complete set of documentation for all identified update processes?

External Dependencies

None.

ANNEXE A – DESCRIPTION OF SYSTEM DEVELOPMENT TEMPLATE

The System Development Template (SDT) provides a common structure for the overall system development process. This template is used extensively in the definition of SSADM.

The System Development Template divides the development process into a number of distinct areas of concern, as shown in the diagram below.

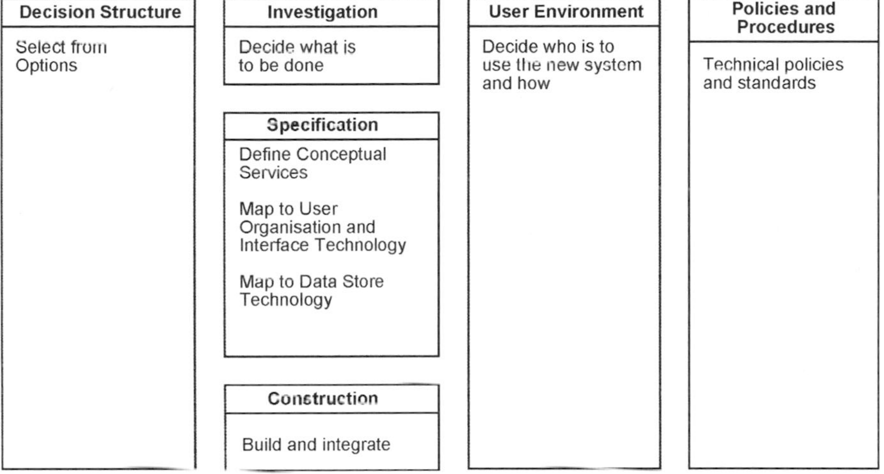

Figure A-1 System Development Template general view

The 3-schema specification architecture (which covers the Specification area) concentrates on those products that will ultimately lead, sometimes via other products, into elements of software. The SDT takes a broader view and divides the system development process into activity areas onto which all the development products may be mapped.

ANNEXE B – DESCRIPTION OF EU-RENT CASE STUDY

EU-Rent is a car rental company owned by EU-Corporation. It is one of three businesses – the other two being hotels and an airline – that each have their own business and IT systems, but share their customer base. Many of the car rental customers also fly with EU-Fly and stay at EU-Stay hotels.

EU-Rent business

EU-Rent has 1000 branches in towns all over Europe. At each branch cars, classified by car group, are available for rental. Each branch has a manager and booking clerks who handle rentals.

Rentals

Most rentals are by advance reservation; the rental period and the car group are specified at the time of reservation. EU-Rent will also accept immediate ('walk-in') rentals, if cars are available.

At the end of each day cars are assigned to reservations for the following day. If more cars have been requested than are available in a group at a branch, the branch manager may ask other branches if they have cars they can transfer to him/her.

Returns

Cars rented from one branch of EU-Rent may be returned to any other branch. The renting branch must ensure that the car has been returned to some branch at the end of the rental period. If a car is returned to a branch other than the one that rented it, ownership of the car is assigned to the new branch.

Servicing

EU-Rent also has service depots, each serving several branches. Cars may be booked for maintenance at any time provided that the service depot has capacity on the day in question.

For simplicity, only one booking per car per day is allowed. A rental or service may cover several days.

Customers

A customer can have several reservations but only one car rented at a time. EU-Rent keeps records of customers, their rentals and bad experiences such as late return, problems with payment and damage to cars. This information is used to decide whether to approve a rental.

Current IT system

Each branch and service depot has a local IT system based on PCs and a file server. The equipment is obsolete and limited in capacity (especially RAM). Hardware failures – screens, disk drives and power supplies – are increasingly frequent. There is currently no use of the Internet either for customer to business communication or for business to business communication.

Application maintainability

The application programs have been maintained over several years. Small RAM in the PCs has necessitated intricate, complex programs which makes amendments progressively more difficult and expensive.

Informal communication

Each location operates almost independently of others. Communication between locations is mainly by phone and fax and co-ordination is very variable. Sometimes, when a car is dropped off at a branch different from the pick-up branch, the drop-off branch will not inform the pick-up branch.

Branch managers tend to co-operate in small groups and not to look for 'spare' cars outside those groups. EU-Rent management feels that some capacity is wasted, but does not have reliable estimates of how much.

Scheduling of service bookings in branch and service depot files is co-ordinated by faxes between branch and depot. Sometimes service bookings are not recorded in the branch files, and cars booked for servicing are rented. Service depots sometimes do not get to know that a car has been transferred to a branch served by other depots until another depot requests the car's service history.

Customer blacklist

A copy of the customer blacklist is held at every branch. It should be updated every week from head office, but the logistics of updating the list with input from 1000 sources and sending out 1000 disks every week are beyond head office's capability. Updates are in fact sent out about every four weeks.

E-Commerce

There is no current use of e-commerce with customers having to phone or fax the individual offices to book cars for rental. This is causing problems in that some competitors have introduced facilities that enable customers to book and monitor their bookings over the Internet and it is thought that this is resulting in a loss of custom.

IT system replacement

EU-Rent management has decided that a new IT system is needed. It is expected whilst the basic operational activity is not expected to change significantly – locations and volume of rentals – it is expected that a number of 'online' systems (e.g. ordering of cars) will be implemented not necessarily as part of the initial role out but shortly thereafter. The new system is justified on three grounds:

- the current system cannot be kept going much longer;
- the perceived need to introduce some online system that can be accessed directly by customers over the Internet;
- better management of numbers of cars at branches and better co-ordination between branches is expected to increase utilisation of cars slightly – the same volume of business should be supportable with fewer cars. Each car ties up about 8,000 Euros in capital and loses about 3,000 Euros in depreciation, so significant savings are possible from small reductions in numbers of cars needed.

Corporate data

After the current IT system has been replaced, EU-Rent management wants to explore possibilities for sharing customer data across the car rental, hotel and airline systems. Even if customers are not stored in a single shared database, it makes sense for all three business areas to have consistent customer information on current address, telephone number, credit rating, etc.

It will be useful to know in each system when there are problems with a customer in other systems. And it may be possible to run promotions in one system, based on what EU-Corporation knows from the other systems about customers.

Future requirements

A customer loyalty incentive scheme is also under consideration. The requirement is not yet precisely defined but the scheme will be comparable with those offered by EU-Rent's competitors.

Members of the scheme will accumulate credit points with each car rental. They will exchange points for 'free' rentals. Only the base rental price will be payable by points; extra charges such as insurance and fuel will be paid for by cash or credit card. When this is introduced it is expected that customers will wish to be able to check (either by the use of a call-centre or directly over the Internet) the current state of their credit points.

Rationale for EU-Rent

The business of EU-Rent is car rentals, but this is largely irrelevant; it merely provides an easily understood context for examples. The business issues and user requirements in EU-Rent could be easily mapped to other systems. They include:

- a requirement to deliver a range of services (rental of cars of different quality and price) at many locations (rental branches), with different volumes of business and patterns of demand;
- customers who may use more than one location, but whose business with the whole organisation should be tracked;
- strong general policies set centrally (car models that may be used, rental tariffs, procedures for dealing with customers), but significant flexibility and authority for local managers (number of cars owned by branch, authority to over-ride published tariff to beat competitors' prices);
- a requirement for customers to be able to directly access aspects of the system;
- performance targets for local managers;
- a requirement for capacity planning and resource replenishment (disposal and purchase of cars, moving of cars between branches); possibilities for this to be managed locally, regionally or centrally;
- locally-managed sharing or swapping of resources or customers between branches to meet short-term unforeseen demand;
- an internal support structure (the maintenance depots) needed to maintain the resources and ensure that the product delivered to customers is of adequate quality;
- a customer base that is shared with other, separate systems (EU-Stay hotels and EU-Fly airline), and possibilities of communicating or co-ordinating with these systems.

Many of these characteristics are common to other types of business; for example, health care, vocational training, social security, policing, retail chain stores, branch banking.

ANNEXE C – GLOSSARY OF TERMS

alternative case

A concept used within Entity Life Histories or any other Jackson-like structure which permits the use of the Quit and Resume convention. The alternative case is a part of the structure which is used only when a quit occurs from the assumed case.

assumed case

A concept used within Entity Life Histories or any other Jackson-like structure which permits the use of the Quit and Resume convention. The assumed case is a part of the structure which is always visited but may be substituted by the alternative case when a quit occurs.

business event

A business event is a trigger which activates one or more business activities.

Business events are of three types:

- external inputs – inputs from outside the system boundary;
- decisions made in business activities within the system;
- scheduled points in time.

A business event may trigger more than one activity. A business activity may be triggered by more than one business event.

Conceptual Process Modelling

Is used to translate the information gathered during Entity Behaviour Modelling into a logical specification of the required processing for events and enquiries which can then be translated into a physical design for the system in any implementation. The precise products of Conceptual Process Modelling may vary depending upon the technical environment of the project.

Conceptual Process Modelling produces Effect Correspondence Diagrams, Enquiry Access Paths, Update Process Models and Enquiry Process Models.

correspondence

A one-to-one relationship between effects or accesses on Effect Correspondence Diagrams and Enquiry Access Paths. There are two types of correspondence:

- single: between two single effects/accesses;
- iterated: between one single effect/access and a 'set of' another effect/access.

A correspondence is directional and will almost always represent an access via a relationship on the Logical Data Model.

death

The state of an entity occurrence which no longer has an active role within the system. Entity occurrences can be interrogated by enquiries. Normally, the next state following death would be deletion.

effect

The set of processing initiated by an event for a single entity.

effect correspondence

A one-to-one relationship between effects. There are two types of correspondence represented by this concept:

- single – between two single effects;
- iterated between one single effect and a 'set of' another effect.

An effect correspondence is directional and will almost always represent an access via a relationship on the Logical Data Model. An effect may be the source of many correspondences but the destination of only one.

Effect Correspondence Diagram

Shows all the effects an event has on entities within the system and how those effects correspond to one other. Operations and conditions can be added to the diagrams to act as a complete specification of the processing required for an event. Where required, Effect Correspondence Diagrams may be transformed into Update Process Models.

effect qualifier

An occurrence of an entity may be affected in one of several mutually exclusive ways by an event. A single occurrence of an event will result in only one type of effect. Each possible effect is separately identified on the Entity Life History diagram by using the event name followed by a description of the effect enclosed in round brackets. This qualifying name is called the effect qualifier.

enquiry

An element which requires information to be read from the Logical Data Model but involves no update processing. Some update functions contain enquiries as well as updates (events).

An enquiry is something that triggers a Conceptual Model process to extract information from the system data.

Enquiry Access Path

The route through the Logical Data Model from an entry point to the entity, or entities, required for a particular enquiry.

Enquiry Process Model

Consists of a Jackson-like structure diagram describing the processing required for an enquiry. The structure is based on the Enquiry Access Path.

enquiry trigger

The data items that must be input to the system to initiate an enquiry.

Entity Access Matrix

A grid that is used to identify which entities are affected by a particular event or accessed by specific enquiries. It provides two checks, that is: that each event/enquiry affects/accesses at least one entity and that each entity is affected by at least one event.

Entity Behaviour Modelling

Entity Behaviour Modelling covers a set of techniques which model the interaction between data and processes in the Conceptual Model. It comprises the techniques Enquiry Identification, Event Identification and Entity Life History Analysis.

Entity Life History

An Entity Life History (ELH) charts all of the events that may cause a particular entity occurrence to change in some way and places them in sequence.

An Entity Life History is a combination of all possible lives for every occurrence of an entity. Each occurrence is constrained to act in the way defined by the Entity Life History for that entity.

Entity Life History Analysis

Part of Entity Behaviour Modelling. The Entity Life History Analysis technique is used to investigate the lives of entities, identifying the events which affect their lives, documenting the way in which the lives are affected and showing the sequence in which the effects take place. The major operations for each effect are identified.

entity role

If a single occurrence of an event affects more than one occurrence of a particular entity and the effects are different, the entity has a different role for each different type of effect. Entity roles are identified by adding them to effect boxes on the Entity Life History enclosed in square brackets. An effect can have both an entity role and an effect qualifier but is more likely to have either one or the other.

event

An event is something that triggers a Conceptual Model process to update the system data. It is usually sourced by an event which occurs in the business environment, notified to the system via one or more functions. An event provides the reason for an update process to be initiated. The name of the event should reflect what is causing the process to be invoked and not the process name itself. Typical event names might include terms such as 'Receipt', 'Notification', 'Decision', 'Arrival', 'New', 'Change' event data.

operation

An elementary piece of processing.

Includes entity operations and function operations:

- an entity operation is used in combination with other operations to make up effects. This concept represents the central definition of an operation which can be referenced by a number of different effects. Each operation will be defined once and referenced wherever it is used (for example, on an Entity Life History, an Effect Correspondence Diagram and Update Process Model);
- a function operation is referenced by Dialogues. Dialogue elements can have function operation identifiers attached to them. Each operation is uniquely identified and the unique identifier is placed in a small soft box under the dialogue element within which it is invoked. There are two different categories of function operation that can be used:
    - data manipulation;
    - validation.

parallel structure

Appearing on Entity Life Histories, this is used to show where certain events will definitely happen within the lifetime of an entity, but not in a prescribed order.

quit and resume

The use of Quit and Resume helps the analyst separate out alternative patterns in an Entity Life History, each of which starts the same way. Quits and Resumes are used to jump from an 'assumed case' to an 'alternative case'. The assumed case is always visited first on the Entity Life History. When an event occurs which shows that the Entity Life History should be in the alternative case, a quit occurs to the appropriate part of the alternative case.

'read-ahead' convention

Convention used in Conceptual Process Modelling products where an iterated access to an entity is indicated. The process reads the first occurrence of the entity before entering the iteration, thus being able to test for its existence and validity before commencing the processing under the iterated components.

state indicator

Each entity has a state indicator, updated each time an event causes an update to the entity's data. A state indicator can be thought of as an additional attribute within each entity. Where there is a need to record that an event has occurred, the state indicator is automatically updated to a new value.

Inspection of the state indicator value of an entity occurrence at any one time will identify where the entity occurrence is within its life, and determine which event(s) may next update the entity occurrence. The validation logic implicit in the state indicators can be carried forward into logical design and built into the processing logic.

State indicators can be used to validate the structure of an Entity Life History. The state indicator values should be consistent with the structure of the Entity Life History diagram. State indicators can be numeric or states can be named.

success unit

Is a set of processing which must succeed or fail as a whole within the system. When a failure occurs the system is restored to the state it was in immediately before the 'success unit' began.

System Development Template

The System Development Template provides a common structure for the overall system development process.

It divides the process into a number of distinct areas of concern:

- Investigation;
- Specification;
- Construction;
- Decision Structure;
- User Organisation;
- Policies and Procedures.

The Specification area contains the Three-schema Specification Architecture which is made up of the areas Conceptual Model, Internal Design and External Design. The Three-schema Specification Architecture concentrates on those products that will ultimately lead, sometimes via other products, into elements of software. The System Development Template takes a broader view. It divides the system development process into activity areas onto which the development products may be mapped.

Update Process Model

Is a structure diagram for the update (event) processing and the associated operations list. This is based on the Entity Life Histories, which provide a data-oriented view of the system, and the associated Effect Correspondence Diagrams, which provide an event-oriented or process-oriented view of the system.

INDEX

A

B

C

D

E

F

G

I

J

K

L

M

N

O

P

Q

R

S

T

U

W